The Artist Entrepreneur

The Artist Entrepreneur

Finding Success in a New Arts Economy

RONALD C. MCCURDY
RICHARD E. GOODSTEIN
ERIC J. LAPIN

ROWMAN & LITTLEFIELD
Lanham • Boulder • New York • London

Published by Rowman & Littlefield
An imprint of The Rowman & Littlefield Publishing Group, Inc.
4501 Forbes Boulevard, Suite 200, Lanham, Maryland 20706
www.rowman.com

6 Tinworth Street, London, SE11 5AL, United Kingdom

British Library Cataloguing in Publication Information Available

Library of Congress Control Number: 2019951013

ISBN 9781538123287

Contents

List of Exercises

Introduction

"The two most important days in your life are the day you are born and the day you find out why."

—*Mark Twain*

Most artists discover the intrinsic desire to pursue a career in the arts at a young age. Many are attracted to the arts because they heard someone play a musical instrument, went to a Broadway show, attended a dance recital, read an inspirational book, or saw a painting, drawing, or sculpting by one of the masters. Whatever the artistic discipline, most artists knew early in their lives that the arts would play a significant role. Often, even those who chose not to pursue the arts professionally remain active in one capacity or another. Former Secretary of State Condoleezza Rice comes to mind as someone who studied music as a child and young adult, but chose a different profession while maintaining her love for music as a concert pianist. Former major league baseball stars Bronson Arroyo (Boston Red Sox) and Bernie Williams (New York Yankees) have both continued to perform their music long after their baseball careers ended. Williams actually earned Grammy nominations following his successful career as a New York Yankee. Even former President George W. Bush has enjoyed developing his love of painting following his years in the White House. It is true that art is something that chooses you; one does not choose to become an artist.

I knew pretty early on that I was going to pursue music as a profession. That's what I wanted to do. I never thought about doing anything else. —Kenny Barron, jazz pianist, composer, and NEA Jazz Master.

Every time I started imagining doing anything else but playing the piano, I would get this dreadful feeling that would wash over me. —Marina Lomazov, international concert pianist and Steinway performing artist.

When did I realize I was going to be an artist? Wow, definitely a different time than I realized I'd be a musician, which was early. —Jeff Coffin, Grammy-winning saxophonist, composer, and educator who has performed as a member of Bela Fleck and the Flecktones and the Dave Matthews Band.

The standard model is for those who are drawn to a career in the arts to typically pursue specialized training through higher education.

ACADEMIC AND ARTISTIC CLIMATE

It has been clear, however, that most colleges and universities are operating in a nineteenth or twentieth-century model, and have not adjusted to the evolving artistic landscape and the modern arts economy. From their perspective, teaching the craft of art is their sole charge. Anything beyond that is the student's responsibility to figure out. Some do, most do not.

But there is a reason to be optimistic. There are tremendous opportunities to create art in today's world due to the explosion of technology and the resultant opportunities to build a career through social media and new live performance venues. The conventional means of pursuing a career is evolving at a rapid pace, and a paradigm shift is required for artists to reinvent how they will shape their own artistic careers. To do so, one must have the tools and a vision for what is possible.

This is not a message of doom and gloom; rather it is a wake-up call to those who need help figuring out ways to expand and create artistic opportunities. It is a message that the new arts economy demands an approach as an Artist Entrepreneur. There are plenty of opportunities for those who have the tenacity to work hard honing their artistic and entrepreneurial skills. Young artists must realize that a failed audition means "not right now," and that while the thought of converting one's art into commerce can be a daunting task, it becomes easier if young artists begin to view themselves as sole proprietors and as entrepreneurs early in the process. By definition, an entrepreneur is someone who organizes a business venture and assumes the risk. As professional artists, we must build a business model to make a living creating art.

In most schools, those who are pursuing arts degrees are taught to become excellent "recreators" of other artists. Artists learn from the masters of their craft, whether it's Picasso, Beethoven, or Monk. This is a good and necessary first step in arts training, but arts education cannot stop there. Especially in higher education, we must do more to guide, help shape artistic leaders, encourage disruptors, and produce Artist Entrepreneurs.

My goal was to play an instrument to the best of my abilities and to be able to make some kind of living doing that.—Marina Lomazov, concert pianist

---

Think of how children are able to play games that allow their imaginations to soar. They create imaginary scenarios and characters in order to build a story. They are only limited by their imagination. This is a form of storytelling and creative thinking that is seldom nurtured as young artists mature. From the time a young student learns to paint, joins a band, participates in a play, or sings in a choir, they are told what songs to sing, what words to say, and what notes to play. The director or conductor decides the program and how the compositions or scenes will be interpreted. Young artists are told when, where, and what to wear for every performance. This continues through college, thus leaving very few (if any) of the creative decisions up to the developing artist. Upon graduation, students typically have never had an opportunity (beyond a senior recital or showcase, and often not even then) to develop the skills needed to be independent contractors and Artist Entrepreneurs. In most cases, students receive degrees without any of the necessary tools to be successful and begin a sustainable career. For the entirety of their college experience, arts students are told or shown what to do next with little thought to career development needs.

To survive and thrive in today's market requires planning and knowledge of how to navigate the incredibly competitive arts economy. The information shared in this book is applicable to anyone who is looking to mount and sustain a career in the arts. The principles and concepts are essentially the same for musicians, actors, or writers because the challenges are the same for dancers, writers, filmmakers, and visual artists. Everyone in the arts has the capacity to engage in this kind of creative and entrepreneurial thinking. However, most find this approach difficult because the creative process is a skill set not typically nurtured in secondary or higher education.

It's become very different than it used to be. The paradigm has absolutely shifted. You want to be a musician, great, but here are some things to think about. Budget to merchandise, to getting folders together if you're playing original music, they have to have the right music, it has to be labeled, it has to be in the right order, it has to have numbers, you have to have contract signed, you have to have hotels, which is the largest expense you're ever going to have on the road, you have to know what your car is getting for gas mileage. If you're getting a rental, how much is that rental? All these different things. So understanding that it is a business. And if you're trying to make money, then you have to have a plan, you have to have a budget, you have to be able to operate in the black, or else you're losing money. So I've always operated on the premise that I'm not losing money. —Jeff Coffin, saxophonist/composer

---

Many parents are often concerned about their children pursuing careers in the arts. As college teachers, we often hear the trepidation in their voices while on campus visits for prospective students and at recruiting events. Most parents want to know if their son or daughter will find work upon graduation or have to return home after four years of college. They are not sure that their children will be able earn a living or have a career as an artist. Our response is to inform parents that the arts, like all careers, offer no guarantees for consistent employment. However, those who are able to mount and sustain careers in the arts are those who are willing to invest the time honing their skills and have a dogged determination to remain vigilant in their quest to have a career as an artist.

Angela Beeching's book *Beyond Talent* is such a profound title. It signals that the twenty-first-century artist will not be allowed to focus solely on talent. That statement alone is one of the most important aspects for the emerging artist to realize—talent will not be enough for today's artist. As students enter colleges, universities, or conservatories, they quickly recognize that everyone admitted is talented. In that moment most students begin to compare how they stack up in comparison to their peers in terms of their talent level. Most university-level arts majors come from high school programs where they were the best. This "big fish, small pond syndrome" is quickly realized at the first audition of the school year. Some students will recognize that they've got work to do in order to compete with their fellow classmates for positions in the orchestra, dance companies, gallery showings, or theatrical productions. Others will become somewhat complacent or disillusioned and not develop much beyond their abilities when they entered as a freshman. To be admitted into some of our top schools confirms that talent is already in place. It now becomes a question of how badly do you, as an artist, want to rise to the top of your chosen field? How much determination and grit do you possess? How much are you willing to be told "no" but still continue to persevere? How broad is your level of creativity to serve as the driver of your own career? How much are you willing to step out of your comfort zones by trying new things and thinking of your work as a business? Are you ready to become an Artist Entrepreneur?

I remember my "big fish, small pond" moment very vividly. I had been the top clarinet player at my high school, top in the county, and one of the top players in the state. Then, on day one in college, all of the students interested in chamber music were supposed to meet in the band room for a reading session. I clearly remember the feeling of panic when I heard the other clarinetists. That feeling has stuck with me and motivated me ever since.—Eric Lapin

---

I had to audition for colleges, I auditioned for Carnegie Mellon's musical theater acting program and got in. I had a really challenging time because it was the first time I was away from home where I had been the star of my theater program and was trying find out who I was as a human being while at the same time being in a conservatory program that was demanding things of me in a different way. And I struggled but ultimately was able to find my way and graduate.—Michael McElroy, Tony nominated actor, singer, music director, educator.

These are the questions every artist must ponder. You may be familiar with the story about the jazz trumpet player, Wynton Marsalis, during his formative years. Wynton happened to be near the bottom of his own high school trumpet section. Of course he had talent, as did most of his peers, but for whatever reason, he had not quite demonstrated that he would become the virtuoso that he is today. Wynton recognized where he stood among his fellow classmates and decided to spend countless hours honing his skills. He had the discipline to sit for hours in a practice room until he perfected a certain technique. He explored his love for classical and jazz music, and later ventured into composition.

One challenging part about being an artist is that you never know how much innate talent the universe has given you. How much growth is due to hard work versus natural ability? We simply don't know. Our hunch is that there is no substitute for hard work. Hard work always trumps talent. Those who have chosen the arts as a profession have elected to pursue a career where there are no guarantees. Unlike those who pursue careers in science, engineering, or the medical field where the job prospects are more immediately favorable, the arts require a different kind of mindset. You embrace art because that is what you were born to do. There is no Plan B. If there is a Plan B, some will be more inclined to take it. As humans, we oftentimes will take the path of least resistance.

There wasn't really any plan B. I remember having conversations with my dad, or he might even call them arguments, and him saying, well I'll pay for college, but you know, you have to at least minor in business. This is it, I'm putting all of my eggs in this basket. This is what I'm doing.
—Jeff Coffin, saxophonist/composer

Although Mozart, Haydn, Beethoven, Charlie Parker, Alvin Ailey, and Michelangelo were all freelance and professional artists, they still had to learn how to parlay their talents into commerce. Most artists do not choose careers in the arts because it will make them rich and famous. Fame and fortune is not, and should not, be the motivation. The goal should be to create and present your art at the highest level. As Dr. Cornel West often states, "one must have a voracious appetite for greatness." If the art is "great" then there's a good chance the fame and fortune will follow. We'll speak more about arts and commerce later.

The impetus for this book is to help aspiring artists gain an edge as they navigate the artistic landscape as a student, recent graduate, or someone who did not attend college. College is certainly not the only route an artist can take. With the high cost of today's college education, aspiring artists need to think carefully before committing to a four-year degree and the potential return on investment. While the lifetime earnings potential for college graduates has proven to be worth almost twice that of a high school graduate, on average, those pursuing a non-traditional arts career such as a country or pop musician or dancer should carefully weigh the benefits a higher education degree can offer.

We make the assumption that those who read this book have aspirations of pursuing a career in the arts. Although, we fully recognize that not everyone who pursues a performance-based degree or aspires to be a professional artist will achieve their goals. However, we suspect there are many who have the skills and technical expertise, but simply lack the necessary knowledge to mount and sustain a career in the arts.

This book is more than a "how to" manual. It is designed to find ways to tap into the creative process and provide tools to mount and present a creative endeavor. It is designed to help the emerging artist think with a different paradigm. In most instances, we have discovered that many students do not think beyond the next concert, performance, play, term paper, recital, or even rehearsal. As a result, graduation in many ways sneaks up on them.

We offer ideas and strategies on how to develop, market, and mount creative ideas. Many students have great ideas, but the challenge becomes how to convert these ideas into art that will warrant repeated performances or showcases. We will expose you to a variety of business-related topics that will facilitate the launching of your artistic career. For example, students should understand the process of creating big ideas. The idea is to craft Big Idea Projects that will gain traction and have a sustained shelf life beyond a senior or graduate recital.

The typical college curriculum never addresses how an artist protects their intellectual property, how artists obtain commissions, how to communicate with arts presenters, book a tour, handle the logistics of a tour, deal with taxes and bookkeeping, understand contracts with gallery owners, or how presenters craft technical riders.

These are just a few topics that go unanswered or even are asked by students who are in college honing their artistic skills. As the saying goes, "we don't know, what we don't know." We certainly concede that not everyone wants this responsibility. Some artists are content to serve as interpreters or participants in the performances of works created by other artists. Their role is to recreate art that has already been composed, choreographed, or designed by someone else. This book is designed for those who have a desire to push the envelope and those who have a strong intrinsic desire to create their own art. All of us have this trait; but some choose to be more proactive than others. Hopefully, some will be inspired by these words and realize that they are limited only by their own imagination and become true Artist Entrepreneurs.

WHY SOME ARTISTS GIVE UP

One of the first empirical studies suggesting career limitations for performance-based students was found in a 2004 longitudinal study conducted by Daniel J. Wakin of the *New York Times*, titled the *Juilliard Effect: Ten Years Later*. In short, the article surveyed Juilliard graduates from the class of 1994 and provided a sobering report on where they ended up. Of the thirty-six Juilliard graduates who were traced, one-third (12/36) were no longer involved in music. Many spoke of being naïve about the music profession, and some became disillusioned and finally decided to pursue other interests. Some just needed a job that allowed them to pay the bills. The article speaks volumes on how, at one of the most respected arts schools in the world, many students were ill-prepared to mount and sustain careers in the arts. While some students simply did not have the "grit" and dedication to make it as performers, the study also indicated that many others simply lacked the knowledge of how and where to mount a career in the arts. This article demonstrated that even Juilliard was operating in a nineteenth or twentieth-century paradigm.

The current question higher education faces is how will today's arts students find a sustainable career in a new arts economy with fewer jobs and a multitude of qualified artists? How will arts graduates thrive or even survive in what is already an overcrowded field of working artists? Is simply being an outstanding performer enough in the twenty-first-century? How is it possible to distinguish your "voice" from the plethora of artists who are vying for the same opportunities? Is it practical to be a performance or studio art major as an undergraduate student? These are questions that many students (and certainly most parents) have pondered to varying degrees for many years. Some see the handwriting on the wall and start planning and building the multiple skills needed for a career in the arts early in the process. Others seem to happily drift through school completely content performing in school ensembles and taking studio classes with little regard for what awaits them upon graduation.

WHAT DOES THIS MEAN?

In today's new arts landscape there are too many students graduating with bachelor's, master's, and doctorates who are unemployed or underemployed within the new arts economy. While the issue of underemployment is not arts-specific according to a Burning Glass and Strada Institute 2017 report, unprepared artists are hit particularly hard in this economic reality. Those who are employed are more than likely scrambling to eke out a living through various freelance, part-time, teaching, and other non-arts related jobs. During times of low unemployment, many performance and conservatory graduates go immediately into another field where they are often less prepared than their peers for a sustainable career path because of the narrowly focused training they received in college.

Once this reality hits home, many arts students take extra classes to become eligible for teaching jobs, change majors, or simply drop out of the arts altogether. The notion of bachelor of arts degrees, arts business classes, entrepreneurship training, and double majors seems to be one answer to this seemingly unstoppable trend.

In the chapters that follow, we will provide theoretical and practical exercises and anecdotal evidence to help you reach your dream of becoming an Artist Entrepreneur.

1

A Model for Success

"Art is what you do, not who you are."

—Herbie Hancock

DEFINING YOURSELF AS AN ARTIST

Artists are very different creatures. We don't view life in the same fashion as the rest of the world. For an artist, to hear birds chirping, the bustling sounds of a large city, or the sounds of rain hitting a window can be the source of a creative idea. An artist observing a beautiful sunset, mountain range, or some magnificent act of nature can be rich source material for a poem, painting, or piece of pottery. For choreographers, leaves blowing in the wind or the angle of a bird's flight path can become the basis for a new dance. In short, artists view the world through a different lens. As artists, our task is to find the beauty, the ugly, the tragedy, and the triumphs in life. Art can address a full range of emotions. In many cases art reflects the strongest emotions we have as humans. That is, love or anger. This may include someone looking for love or pining over a lost love. It could reflect the love someone has for a parent, sibling, friend, a pet, or nature. Art can also reflect the darker side of the human experience such as war or the genocide of a particular population or ethnic group. The bottom line is that art is a reflection of and interpretation of life.

Artists delight in investing significant parts of their lives honing their artistic skills. We have what we call the "seagull syndrome." If you've ever observed seagulls at the beach, they are constantly looking for food. Rarely do you ever find sea gulls just "hanging out." They're working! There are no days off! This is the life of an artist.

The artist, sculptor, painter, architect, and poet Michelangelo would famously spend all of his time focused on his art. He would even forget to eat meals when particularly focused on a project! While focus and concentration is important, we have to remember to take care of ourselves.—Eric Lapin

---

I didn't want someone else to be responsible for my artistic growth.—Michael McElroy, actor

---

Career opportunities for performing artists have changed significantly over the past twenty-five years. For aspiring professional musicians, the days of touring big bands, steady orchestral jobs, or full-time teaching positions are largely over. In addition, recording studio work is nearly nonexistent, most live, film, and television music comes out of a box, and touring Broadway gigs are rare and largely replaced with reduced orchestras dominated by rhythm players and synthesizers. For actors, designers, and other theater and dance professionals, the same diminished career opportunities are also now a reality. And for visual artists, selling a piece of art, one work at a time, is a daunting prospect. Short-term contracts, commercial opportunities, and living project-to-project is the norm. While the growth of artistic outlets and creative opportunities in television and digital mediums have skyrocketed in recent years due to the proliferation of streaming networks, arts education within higher education has not kept pace with current job opportunities.

In parallel with this reduction of traditional career opportunities and the proliferation of quality arts schools, there have never been so many aspiring artists trying to carve out a career as professional artists. According to a 2015 College Music Society report, the number of baccalaureate degrees awarded in the visual and performing arts increased by 123 percent between 1991 and 2011.

Simply put, the art professions have a supply and demand problem: there is more of a supply of talent than there is demand for viable jobs and a sustainable career. The question becomes, how are arts graduates going to pay the rent and eat, and where are these talented and gifted young artists going to have a chance to present their art and forge a career? What options do they have?

Many students interested in the arts begin their journey in grade school and continue through middle school, high school, and then into college. They take art classes, participate in band, orchestra, community theaters, and choir, learn to write and tell stories and poems, or take dance classes. Some also take classes in the visual arts or perhaps were involved in school plays or musicals. Arts participation was an attractive alternative to sports and, for many students, offered a sense of community that resonated with many teenagers. Arts participation is also about having fun (which obviously should remain).

Students prepared for school concerts, theatrical plays, dance recitals, musical festivals, solo and ensemble competitions, and art exhibits, while likely not thinking of becoming a professional artist. It was simply done for fun, to be a part of a collective, and to present their art to their respective communities. Over time, however, many students begin to understand and hone their level of artistic ability and develop a passion and a desire to pursue advanced training in their art.

Talented arts students are identified early and subsequently recruited by colleges, universities, and conservatories to serve as artists in their respective programs. The more talented students are often offered significant tuition discounts (scholarships) based on skill. As students start to better understand the complexity and realities of an arts education, they begin to consider how they can make a living, or at least make money for something that has brought them so much passion and pleasure. At this point, many begin seeing how the professional world differs from their collegiate experiences. For example, students spend weeks preparing for one concert or a play or art exhibition, only to repeat that cycle several times throughout their academic careers. On occasion, there might be an opportunity for students to pick up summer stock work, church jobs during the holiday seasons, a pit orchestra gig, a commercial art commission, or a jazz student will find a club date here and there; but these experiences hardly represent the true career preparation that a student needs to build and sustain a career in the arts. The result is that arts students often change majors, add a dual major or an education track, and/or suddenly realize that four years has elapsed and they have significantly developed their talent, but have no idea how to transition their artistic training and four-year degree into a sustainable career as an artist.

"FEAR-BASED EDUCATION"

As many students come to the end of their tenure as an undergraduate student, some feel as if they're not quite ready to venture into the "real world" or don't have any job prospects, so they decide to attend graduate school. Jazz bassist and educator John Clayton calls this *Fear-Based Education*. This pattern often continues when the same student completes their master's degree and decides to pursue a doctorate. John is certainly not advocating against students pursuing an advanced arts degree, just that there should be a clear understanding for *why* an advanced degree is being pursued. His argument (and we agree) is that venturing into graduate school should only be a last resort when no other options are available or when it specifically addresses your career goals.

Many times this pattern occurs because the young artist is afraid to "go for it." Because fear creeps in, graduate school becomes the safe option. Students need to truly understand the potentially limited return on investment, time, and cost of a graduate degree. With the ever-increasing cost of higher education, students need to carefully weigh the costs vs. returns on a multi-year delay on entering the workforce and adding the long-term debt that an advanced degree might create. Highly talented students often are encouraged by their mentors and teachers to consider a graduate degree to continue to hone their skills and bring needed maturity to their craft. Often this encouragement is accompanied by significant financial commitments to the student in the form of graduate assistantships and talent-based scholarships, which perpetuates the cycle of too many qualified graduates for too few jobs.

We have each witnessed this phenomenon our entire careers in higher education and have even been guilty ourselves:

I am qualified to speak to this matter so honestly because I am guilty myself of having done the exact same thing. I completed my undergraduate degree and immediately started my master's and then my doctorate. While I am grateful that I completed all three degrees, the truth of the matter is that I had no idea what shape my career would take. I literally backed into my first college teaching position because I worked hard and basically created a position for myself. That is a path that I certainly would not recommend for others to emulate. In short, I was lucky. The stars just happened to all line up for me. Like most undergraduates, I had no idea what was next, so grad school was a wonderful way to remain in my comfort zone and delay the inevitable. Finding a job!—Ron McCurdy

---

I finished my undergraduate degree in clarinet performance with very little idea of what I was going to do next. So, I settled into the family business. I was working at my family's ice cream shop while teaching a few lessons and playing a few gigs on the side. Despite having no knowledge or understanding of arts administration, I finally got up the courage to contact the local symphony orchestra about any possible internship opportunities. Thankfully, an internship turned into a low paying, part-time job. However, there wasn't much room to grow at the orchestra, and fear about my next step set in. So, I went back to grad school with very little plan for my artistic future. —Eric Lapin

As a high school senior, I wanted to be principal clarinet in the New York Philharmonic. It was my first few weeks as an undergraduate that I realized that I was no longer the best clarinetist in school. In fact, I sat in the middle of the section and saw that my dream to move to New York wasn't realistic as I had always been "king of the hill" in high school. I quickly changed my major to music education, but without having any real desire (at that time) to teach or being presented other viable career options as an eighteen-year-old. My music education was nothing but a safety net at the time. —Rick Goodstein

THE TWENTY-FIRST-CENTURY ARTIST

Justin DiCioccio, former dean and director of jazz studies at the Manhattan School of Music in New York, suggests that anyone hoping to have a career in today's music profession should possess the following traits: *performer*, *composer*, and *pedagogue*. We've added yet another trait: *intellectual*. Let's take a moment to examine each of these traits.

Without question, a budding professional artist needs to have the requisite skills of the highest caliber. That should be a given. This is where hours are invested daily to perfect the ability and skills to present art at the highest level. Artists practice technique for hours on end, learn repertoire, study masterworks, and basically do whatever is necessary to be at the top of their artistic game. The perfection of technique allows the artist to "speak" with expression and clarity. DiCioccio's ideas also insist that every artist engage in some form of composition (e.g., musical score, choreography, novel, script, etc.). Many master teachers have spoken about the discovery of one's "voice" via composition. While not everyone will compose symphonies, string quartets, Broadway showtunes, a novel, jazz standards, or write a compelling script or score for a play, the important thing is for everyone to make a concerted effort to create art.

DiCioccio also believes that every artist will be a pedagogue at some point in their artistic life. Whether we seek to educate audiences through our work, or work as arts educators, we need to be prepared for this critically important mandate as a professional.

I recall once attending an international conference where a major artist had been asked to present a clinic. There were roughly 500 people in attendance waiting to be enlightened. The master teacher (who shall remain nameless) walked up to the mic and said, "Does anybody have any questions?" That was his prepared masterclass! Because of this person's brilliance, he eventually played his instrument and was able to not only salvage, but mesmerize the audience with his brilliance. However, most of us are not able to function at that high level. I suspect that same person would have a problem maintaining classes that met on an ongoing basis. —Ron McCurdy

---

I graduated with a music education degree from a well-respected university, but found that the first five years of my career as a high school teacher were mostly trial and error, with my students being the guinea pigs in my successes and epic failures. (My first teaching assignment included teaching class guitar—I only knew 3 basic chords at the time!) It wasn't until I returned to graduate school (with a wife and new baby) that I began to think seriously about a career in music and to think beyond that of a frustrated performer. —Rick Goodstein

---

Lastly, the twenty-first-century artist must be an intellectual. This helps to ensure that the artist is a citizen of the planet and a critical thinker. Artists should read a variety of books, newspapers, and magazines and stay in tune with current trends in arts and culture, both nationally and internationally. They should attend plays and visit museums and libraries on a regular basis. Current events and a keen sense of history will help artists navigate today's world of 24/7 news, extraordinary political and cultural polarization, and a devaluing of the traditional arts industries. In short, successful artists are curious about many topics. These ingredients provide the makings of a great artist and great art—a successful storyteller. For artistic stories to have the kind of depth and breadth necessary for today's arts climate, it is imperative that the intellectual qualities be part of the equation.

For me, I bring my heart to Dave Matthews, which is my main source of income, but I also teach at Vanderbilt University now for the last 4 years. I do a lot of music clinics around the country, so I can bring my artistry to all these different areas, retain who I am as an artist, but also make money. — Jeff Coffin, saxophonist/composer

---

WHAT IS REQUIRED?

At the highest level, everyone is talented. Therefore, other ingredients are necessary for today's artist to excel. In Stephen Covey's book, *The 7 Habits of Highly Effective People*, the first habit mentioned is *Be Proactive*. This is applicable to every aspect of life and profession including the arts. As an artist, you must become an initiator—a creator. You must engage in activities that will encourage others to present or commission your art. Part of becoming an initiator involves having a *vision* for your art. Covey also encourages his readers to envision the end of your creation at the beginning.

Having a short-term and long-term vision for your art and career is crucial. It is important to regularly write down your short-term and long-term goals. You might tape them to your wall, post them in the shower (as one of my son-in-laws does), or in a pocket notebook à la Jim Snidero. It is important to revisit these goals regularly as they will often change and that's okay. Think of these written goals as a work in progress. This kind of vision is also applicable for creating one's art. Try imagining at the beginning what the final work of art will resemble once it is completed. Imagine in what venue it will be performed or presented and who will be working with you. In short, try to imagine as much detail as possible. This will help as you begin creating and mounting your work. We'll expand on the process of setting goals later in this chapter.

Another one of Covey's habits addresses *Leadership* versus *Management*. Both of these habits are essential to an artist as well. Covey states: "Leadership is primarily a high powered, right brain activity. It's more of an art; it's based on a philosophy." Management is more of a left-brain activity: how do you organize your life? How do you make sure the trains run on time? This has more to do with management. As an artist, this is a must as you begin organizing your schedule for creating, touring, rehearsals, business matters, etc. We'll spend more time addressing both of these items in later chapters.

Covey also discusses the importance of having a *Win-Win* attitude, this is especially true if you're working in an arts ensemble or in a collaborative situation. Human nature forces us to become competitive at times, which can lead to destructive behavior. Egos can easily emerge, become bruised, and subsequently destroy the chemistry of a group. The goal should always be to find ways to create art in a positive environment where everyone feels valued and appreciated. Oftentimes, while a group leader is vetting talent, they will ask, "What kind of person is Sally? Does she play well with others? Does she show up on time? Does she take care of business once she arrives?" If the response from a trusted colleague is not positive, that can make the difference between being hired or passed over for someone else.

Finally, the most important trait of an emerging artist is the ability to *Stick and Stay*. How much determination do you have? Are you willing to work at honing your craft when others are relaxing? Being an artist is not easy. There will be times when you have worked extremely hard to create a work of art, but no one seems interested in booking your show, or you receive a negative review in the newspaper, or experience low attendance at your shows.

As an aspiring conductor/music educator, I could not find a job upon completing my undergraduate degree. In desperation, I ended up taking a job at a high school where I taught guitar, show choir, concert choir and the band with 24 students enrolled. Although I only knew three chords on a guitar and had never sung in a choir, it was the best job for me at the time and allowed me to develop my skills, focus on what I needed to do to reach my goals and pushing through obstacles that seemed impossible to overcome. In hindsight, it was the best 5-year apprenticeship I could ever have imagined. —Rick Goodstein

---

The popular rock funk group, Snarky Puppy, had been trying for years to gain success. They played before many empty clubs and concert halls while their leader, Michael League, "maxed" out several credit cards to keep the group financially afloat. Now, they are playing all of the major festivals worldwide, have a massive following and play to packed audiences, all while winning four Grammys.

Think about the writer J. K. Rowling of the Harry Potter series. She was rejected by twelve publishers before Harry Potter was finally accepted. Misty Copeland was told repeatedly that she did not have the right body size and shape before becoming the principal dancer at the American Ballet Theatre. These are but a few examples of artists who refused to accept "no" for an answer.

We were recently with a group of students who had the chance to meet and talk to Fei Fei, the highly acclaimed classical pianist. The students could not believe that Fei Fei still practiced eight hours a day. Truly "stick and stay." If it were easy, everyone would do it! As an artist, you will be told "no" far more times than you will hear "yes."

IT'S NOT ABOUT THE MONEY—YET!

Once a student was asked, "why do you want to pursue being an artist?" The student responded by saying, "I want to be rich and famous!" The student's response was their attempt to be sarcastic, but there was a sense of innocence, sprinkled with a dosage of post-adolescence delusion. Although it is certainly nice to have the notoriety while reaping the benefits of financial security, most artists do not initially begin an arts career to make them rich and famous. One becomes an artist because that "little voice" inside reminds you that this is what you were born to do. There is no Plan B—honing your skills as an artist is the first thing you think of in the morning and the last thing you think of before you go to sleep! This might sound somewhat fanatical and utopian, but that is the kind of dedication that is required. There is a reason why there is only one Michael Jordan, Mikhail Baryshnikov, Ella Fitzgerald, Wynton Marsalis, J. K. Rowling, and Frank Gehry. What do each of these individuals have in common? They all were dedicated to their craft long before there was any hint of becoming rich and famous. With ready access to social media, it is easy for emerging artists to see the glitz and glamour of becoming a "superstar." This is especially true when some of the music, talent, and dance reality shows offer such a skewed version of reality and the commitment necessary to becoming an artist.

There are examples of some contestants on these reality shows who were working in fast foods one minute and the next moment, they are signing a million-dollar contract. While it is possible for that to occur, it is highly unlikely. A friend of ours tells the story of riding in and living out of a van as a member of Richard Carpenter's band going from gig to gig until the hit single, "Close to You," hit the charts and the band literally went from living out of a van to flying in a Lear jet. Unfortunately, for most artists, dreams of becoming an overnight success are typically unrealized.

The formative years of an emerging artist should be spent honing their skills with an eye toward becoming a professional artist—that is, being paid for your art.

Having a mentor is perhaps one of the most important aspects of this development. Your mentor should be someone who in their own right has experienced a great deal of success in their professional career. They will also be someone who will tell you the truth. Sometimes the most productive conversations with a mentor will have little to do with the actual craft of your art, but will entail life's lessons that will help you to become a more skilled and authentic storyteller. If the art is honest, thoughtful, well-crafted, and compelling, then usually the financial benefits more than likely will follow. It is important to note that creativity should not be approached with the idea that you should write, compose, or perform in a certain manner to gain crowd approval. Crowd approval should not be the motivation for creating your art. Imagine if Picasso, Beethoven, Duke Ellington, Alvin Ailey, or Miles Davis had created their art with the intention of trying to please the public. More on this idea later.

Like many students who decided to attend graduate school because no other option seemed viable, I found myself at the University of Kansas to pursue my master's degree in music. David Baker had been invited to present a series of lectures to the students and faculty at the university. I had never seen someone who was so well versed as a scholar, composer, lecturer and all around great human being. It was at that moment, I decided during my first year of graduate school that this was someone I wanted to emulate. I began to attend the Jamey Aebersold jazz camps where David Baker had taught for years. I took advantage of every opportunity to be in David Baker's presence. I would even go to Bloomington, Indiana, where David taught at Indiana University. I read all of his books and articles and listened to many of his compositions. I appreciated the versatility of David Baker and the fact that he saw something in me that I did not see in myself. We remained close friends and he served as my mentor for more than thirty years. I would often tell him, "no you, no me!"—Ron McCurdy

---

Probably one of my first real mentors was Dizzy Gillespie. Him being a mentor was not in the sense that I studied with him, rather, how much I observed him. There was a lot of non-musical stuff of how he treated people.—Kenny Barron, jazz pianist

You meet people sometimes (Dave Pietro) and you feel like you've known them 1,000 years, when it's only been an hour. He was one of those people for me. Like attracts like. I'm not sure what it is.—Jeff Coffin, saxophonist/composer

WHAT IS AN ARTIST ENTREPRENEUR?

By definition, an entrepreneur is someone who engages in the art of innovation and risk-taking for profit in business. It is becoming increasingly evident that artists need to do whatever they can to take personal control of their careers. Even those who are fortunate enough to secure management or an agent early in their careers should have more than a cursory knowledge and understanding of how their careers and artistic output can be monetized and the business aspects of being a professional. To be an effective Artist Entrepreneur, one must be fluent in both artistic and business matters. As stated earlier, the challenge every artist faces is to parley what you enjoy doing into a career. The operative word in this definition is "risk-taking." Each time an artist steps on stage, paints a landscape, writes a script, or creates a film, they are taking a risk. As artists, we allow ourselves to become vulnerable by sharing our stories and a portion of ourselves with the public. The same kind of vulnerability we experience as an artist, we also face as we create and launch our projects. We don't always know if a particular project will be well-received. We will discuss in more detail later how to better navigate the business side of the artistic landscape.

SELF-EVALUATION—HOW DO YOU MEASURE UP?

This is perhaps one of the most important ingredients to measure how you're progressing as an artist. Do you initiate artistic opportunities or do wait until you are called by someone else for an opportunity? Are you part of the local artistic community? Do you regularly attend other artistic events presented by your colleagues and peers? Are you constantly evaluating the quality of your own artistic creations? Do you ask for constructive feedback of your art? Are you an effective self-critic and/or do you listen to others whose opinion you value? These are some of the questions every artist should ponder.

Successful artists should find a balance between practicing the craft of your art, promoting your art, keeping current in your field, and maintaining personal/family life. The importance of maintaining a healthy work/life balance is extraordinarily important to building and maintaining an artistic career.

There's an old saying, "if you're not moving forward, then you're probably moving backward." There is much truth to that statement. We're reminded of how most major companies operate in terms of rolling out new products. For example, while Apple introduces a new iPhone or computer, you can rest assured that at least three or four generations of the next iPhone are already in development. The same is true with the Walt Disney Company. While some new dimension of the amusement park is under construction, there are plans already in the process to create the next phase of expansion. Another great example is the Coca-Cola Company, they have a world-class marketing division with a laser focus not only on selling more of their existing products, but also being on the lookout for the next product and other new opportunities to build on their distribution model and customer base. This same kind of forward thinking (on a much smaller scale) can be adopted by creative artists. As you launch one of your projects, there should be at least three or four other projects that are at various stages of production. This is what we mean by moving forward. By the time one of your project's shelf-life has expired, you have another project that is ready to be unveiled.

You have to visualize what you did today and that will affect what you're going to do five years later, and how are you going to set up today in a way that's most beneficial long term. It's like a chess game. You set up for the future. You need to be at least two or three moves ahead. —Marina Lomazov, concert pianist

---

SETTING GOALS AND ACHIEVING THEM

It is important that every artist have a list of goals. We suggest that there be two sets of goals, those that are short-term (three to six months) and long-term goals (five and ten years). Think of these goals as a work in process. We suggest that goals be written, printed, and placed where they are regularly visible as a reminder of your aspirations. These goals will and should evolve as you grow as an artist. As you craft these goals, it is equally important to list how you plan to achieve them. For example, if one of your goals is to dance with the American Ballet Theatre, you should have a series of steps you will execute as you implement your plan. Part of your plan may include attending several "live" performances and possibly meeting the artistic director. You might ask to meet with the person who will be in position to one day hire you. These types of meetings are important because they give you an opportunity to forge a personal relationship with a possible future mentor and expand your network. In many ways, this is an audition of sorts, a chance for you to share your thoughts while allowing your desire to become an artist known to your potential mentor. We cannot underestimate the importance of expanding your network of professionals in your field and forging a mentor/mentee relationship with artists you respect. These network and mentor relationships will help you accelerate your career in ways that you once thought were impossible.

It's about doing certain steps, in a certain order. I wish that I had learned all of these things sooner. I wish I realized the importance of playing with the Boston Pops and having a review in the Boston Globe *and how important that part is, sooner, rather than later. I wish I realized the importance of performing "live" broadcasts on the radio to the best of your ability.*—Marina Lomazov, concert pianist

---

Some might call this luck, which by definition for an artist is when opportunity and preparation collide. Others may say that you are creating your own luck by opening doors and building networks.

2

What's the Story?

Finding Your Soul

Artists are storytellers. Much of what we do is tell or interpret a story in a compelling manner. Whether it's a Mozart symphony, painting a scene, acting, creative writing, working behind the scenes on a play, performing a ballet, interpreting a jazz standard, designing a set, or writing a song, you and your audience go on a shared journey. The success of a creative artist is often dependent on how convincingly you craft your story.

In this chapter, we offer you specific exercises and tools that will help open your ability to create art. How do you find your creative voice? What is your story, your raison d'être? How will you tell your story and what are you trying to say?

Throughout history, in great art—art that stands the test of time—an emotional response is elicited from the audience. Great artists are master storytellers who create at such a high level that they tell their stories with effortless conviction. Their storytelling is believable, passionate, and presented with an undeniable sense of purpose. One of the prerequisites for the creation of great art is mastery of the basic tools of the trade—flawless technique and the understanding of the vocabulary and history of art. It's no different than a master carpenter who doesn't think twice when using a hammer or a surgeon who knows every inch of your anatomy. There are no shortcuts. If you haven't mastered the basics and understand the context and history, you won't have much success telling your story and subsequently great art will be beyond your reach.

As a PhD student, I recall one of my professors leading a discussion of the aesthetics of great art as interpreting the world through the lens of the art- ist. He stated that art that achieves an aesthetic level of excellence will lead an audience to understand the world in new or different ways. An artist's ability to pull on personal experiences coupled with technical mastery and a passionate delivery will have a greater ability with which to tell or interpret a convincing story.—Rick Goodstein

In 1913, the premiere of Stravinsky's transformational ballet, the *Rite of Spring*, broke so many conventional rules of the day, many in the audience were unable to process the artistic vision and a near riot famously broke out. In hindsight, we now understand that this creative work reinvented an art form. There is no doubt that both Stravinsky and choreographer Nijinsky knew their craft and were making an artistic statement—a "big idea!" Their story was compelling, and far ahead of its time. While this is a unique case, history is full of artists who have been labeled "ahead of their time." Think about people like John Coltrane, Frank Zappa, Picasso, the Velvet Under ground, van Gogh, Bach, or Frank Lloyd Wright. Can you think of others who relate to you as transformational artists?

Successful artists cannot be hindered by technical limitations or by a lack of a historic perspective. Technical limitations will only hinder the creative process. An artist needs to effortlessly hold the tools of the trade to be suc- cessful. This is one success of the current higher education undergraduate teaching approach—a deep dive into the technical craft of your art. The basic higher education curriculum model also provides a laser-focus on art within the continuum of history and a chronological review of art.

What the typical undergraduate art training does not provide students are opportunities to develop the aesthetic and creative tools necessary to build a sustainable career. Since we know that artists are storytellers and a great storyteller has the ability to take you on a journey that can suspend time, one missing piece of creativity development is an understanding of flow theory and its importance to the creative process.

Hungarian psychologist and former chair of the Psychology Department at the University of Chicago, Mihály Csikszentmihalyi convincingly wrote of how time can seemingly stand still when you are in the "flow." His flow theory talks of musicians and artists optimizing their creative energy when, seemingly, everything else stands still.

Being in the flow might also occur as an audience member. Have you ever attended a concert, watched a movie, or attended a gallery showing and were so transformed by the art that two hours passed in the blink of an eye? These are examples of being in the "flow"—thus great storytelling, and great art.

Throughout the remainder of this book, we will give you exercises that will help you build some skills that are necessary for retooling your approach to an arts career.

Exercise 2.1: Write down 3 examples of when you, as an audience member, have been "in the flow."

---

(1) The first time I listened to the Seiji Ozawa recording of Stravinsky's The Rite of Spring *with the Chicago Symphony Orchestra. (2) Watching* Swan Lake *performed by the Moscow City Ballet. (3) Walking through the halls of The Hermitage and Winter Palace museum in St. Petersburg, Russia.*—Eric Lapin

---

---

(1) At my first Chicago Transit Authority concert as a teenager, the concert was over in a blink of an eye and it helped foster a love of horn bands that has continued to this day.—Rick Goodstein

---

The same can be true for not only audience members, but also the creators of art who become immersed in "the moment" as you draw a painting, write a poem, choreograph a dance, write a song, or perform. The creative process requires immersing ourselves into the art to experience the flow momentum.

Exercise 2.2: Think of 3 times when, as a performer, writer, or artist, you have been in the "flow."

---

(1) My first performance of the Mozart Clarinet Concerto. (2) A college performance of Stravinsky's Rite of Spring. *(3) High school marching band performance at the Lower State Championship.*—Eric Lapin

---

(1) Marching the 5 ½ mile Rose Bowl parade route as one of the directors of the United Way Centennial All-Star Marching Band. (2) After years of working, when I get "in the flow," I can write a complex business-related policy statement or memorandum in what feels like minutes.—Rick Goodstein

Beethoven famously struggled with each turn of a phrase while Mozart would conceptualize an entire symphony, seemingly effortlessly. Similarly, many sculptors see the end result in a block of marble, while others struggle and adjust as they go. As artists, regardless of the medium, we need to be able to open our minds to the creative process and get into a flow state. For some, it's a painful, laborious, time-consuming process, while for others, the process appears to pour out of their bodies effortlessly. Regardless, getting the process started and letting your creative juices flow is the ultimate goal. Teachers of creative writing often tell students who are facing writer's block to just write something—anything. Just start writing. What is true for writers is true of any of the creative arts—just get started.

Great art is often thought of as withstanding the test of time; however, conceptualizing and creating art is personal and the beauty of the creative arts is in the moment. What one perceives as great art is extraordinarily individual, as it should be. Coming to a self-realization of who you are as a person is a crucial step in the development of your creative and artistic expression. These next two exercises will help you focus on both your past and present in order to develop your artistic voice. These exercises may take some time, and require "homework," but are crucial steps in understanding who you are and finding your inner creativity.

Exercise 2.3: Gather information about your family and your roots. Go back several generations and write down your genealogy, your family tree. You or someone in your family may already have this information, but it is important that you write it down, make detailed annotations and collect personal stories.

In this informal development of your artistic "DNA," you will begin to understand who you are and how you got here. Again, to drive home the point, understanding who you are and where you come from will help you develop your skills as a creative artist.

For example, if you have extended family members available, you may want to conduct interviews in order to understand your roots and background. This should be a lot of fun and will provide an amazing insight as to who you are and help you find your artistic voice. Besides first-person research, you may also want to utilize one of the many genealogy resources that are online and other digitized resources that are now available (like Ancestry.com). At the end of this process, you will have a document that should inform you as an artist and serve as a valuable documented history of your family background.

The newly popular and relatively inexpensive DNA and genetic testing, such as 23andMe and MyHeritageDNA, have revealed rich material for artists to explore their background and ancestry that can provide new source material for their work.—Rick Goodstein

---

I grew up in a very musical family. My mom played the piano, my brother, my sister, my uncle, and now all my nieces and nephews, so I grew up in the church. My grandfather started my church so all my family were the musicians and singers in the church. So I always grew up around gospel music but also there was a love of music, period. Mom grew up as a classical pianist and my uncle was a musical theatre director but also a classical pianist. So I grew up with all different types of music in my place, in my home.—Michael McElroy, actor

---

The SWOT analysis is an acronym for "Strengths," "Weaknesses," "Opportunities," and "Threats" and is a basic strategic planning tool for businesses that will work to develop your artistic voice. The SWOT analysis can be a four-block worksheet where you self-identify personal traits that fit each category. You will find that the initial input is easy; but that once you dig into the details, you may find that some of your strengths are actually weaknesses and that may present some opportunities and challenges. This is part of the self-reflection and personal analysis and it allows you to understand your potential as an artist, and perhaps also some of your limitations. There is no doubt that this exercise will reveal much about how you can build upon your strengths and avoid some of your weaknesses all while taking full advantage of opportunities.

A SWOT exercise can be extraordinarily revealing. If you have a partner, spouse, friend, or relative whom you feel completely comfortable with, share some of your self-identified traits and ask for their input. Our belief is that this "360-degree" analysis might unlock some artistic potential and open some creative doors that you hadn't previously considered.

Exercise 2.4: Build a personal SWOT analysis. That is, develop a chart of your Strengths, Weaknesses, Opportunities, and Threats.

With your genealogy and SWOT analysis behind you, it is now time to build a vision statement. This is a crucial step in your development as an artist and should be formed based on the examination of your DNA and SWOT analysis. This exercise will have you develop a one-page statement of artistic purpose. This "Mission Statement" will communicate your work as an artist and serve as a guidepost for your creative endeavors. Can you define your overarching artistic values, what makes you distinctive, and your motivations?

Exercise 2.5: Write a personal artistic mission statement in less than 300 words. It's important that you think this through, to articulate on paper who you are as an artist, what is important to you, and what your artistic values are. This will help you find your voice as an artist and develop your unique perspective on your art.

It is important that every artist have an artistic vision for the creation and implementation of their art. It is my belief that artists have a fiduciary responsibility to tell stories that are truthful, and compelling. —Ron McCurdy

Finding your artistic voice through a personal SWOT analysis, a genealogy study, and a personal artistic mission statement are three tools that will help you to tell your story from a personal perspective. These exercises will set you apart from the thousands of artists who have the talent, drive, and determination but lack an aesthetic core and a self-defined artistic vision. Developing your personal artistic voice, your passion, and your story is the single most powerful tool you can hold as you develop as an artist.

As all professional artists know, this is not an easy arts economy we are attempting to navigate. There are tremendously talented artists who are just as motivated, passionate, and hungry. So how do you stand out, how do you distinguish yourself, how do you develop the artistic charisma needed to get noticed?

IT'S ALL ABOUT YOUR ATTITUDE

The fact is that there are many tremendously talented artists, musicians, actors, and dancers, and one trait that can set you apart beyond talent is a positive attitude. We have learned this through years of experience in many different sectors of the arts economy. When you present yourself as someone other artists want to work with, work will come your way. There are too many talented artists who simply "phone it in." As aspirational professional artists, we need to look for any edge we can muster. A positive attitude of "winning friends and influencing people" (Dale Carnegie) is a must in our competitive economy.

We have interviewed and auditioned literally thousands of prospective members of the Walt Disney All-American College program over the past thirty years. We have seen amazing talent come through the doors and go on to careers at the highest level of our industry. What often distinguishes those who "make it" from those who don't is a "can do" attitude that pairs great talent with a positive outlook on music, life, and the world in general. Through years of experience, we can generally tell in just a few moments if a prospective band member has the talent to be successful. Once this assessment is complete, we spend the rest of the audition time judging the intangibles—how a prospect might react under pressure, what motivates them, and any red flags that might pop up. Undoubtedly, the ability to maintain a positive attitude within an extraordinarily stressful audition environment is the most telling trait that separates those who are hired and those who aren't. Those who are hired are, in every case, those whom we want to spend time with. Our litmus test is to ask ourselves if we want to spend the summer with this prospect.—Rick Goodstein and Ron McCurdy

---

Your positive, unselfish, and honest attitude will get you further than just talent alone. Yes, talent is a prerequisite for a professional artist; however, an unburdened enthusiasm and positive approach to your "job" will take you places that talent alone cannot. Attitude is a decision and choice about how you present yourself, and one of the few skills you can control.

Other traits that are crucial elements of finding your artistic voice and a sustainable career are grit and determination. We've all heard stories of people who have auditioned many times for a gig, submitted countless manuscripts, or proposed multiple project designs only to be turned down at every turn. In the creative arts, unfortunately, this is often true. Grit and determination are characteristics that will serve you well on your way to becoming an artist. You should approach each rejection as not a "no," but a "not yet."

Before joining higher education, I worked in operations and personnel for a regional symphony orchestra. One of my jobs was to assist with the orchestra's audition procedures. At audition after audition, I would hear musicians perform beautifully only to lose out in the end . . . and in orchestral auditions, there is no prize for second place. Talent wasn't quite enough. The artists with the right mix of talent, grit, and determination were the ones who were ultimately successful. —Eric Lapin

---

We have hired a number of prospects who came back for their second or even third audition. While their art and sight-reading have likely improved, the unmistakable grit and determination show through from their persistence and perseverance. In fact, we recently heard of a musician who auditioned for a military band position thirteen times before being hired! —Rick Goodstein and Ron McCurdy

---

As artists, we need to have a deep and unwavering passion for our art. You can't fake it. If that passion isn't there you will find yourself in an artistic "black hole" that will soon make your life as an artist untenable and you will likely become the proverbial starving artist.

Consider, for example, Broadway actors, pit musicians, choreographers, or designers. These professionals make their art come to life eight times a week. Performing the same role or playing in a pit orchestra eight times a week is a remarkable feat; a great example of passionate art making (and being a professional). The unselfish act of putting every ounce of your artistic soul into your artwork night after night is one of the great lessons we must learn as artists. Those of us who understand that every audience is new at every performance and deserve the best of our art will be better equipped to enjoy a successful and fulfilling life as a professional artist. Think of this grit and determination as a work ethic on steroids.

Being told "no" is part of our lives as artists. From every audition rejection to not making the top ensemble or first chair or not having a piece accepted for an exhibition, being rejected is part of our artistic lives. Those artists who go on to "make it" are those who double down and work harder for the next opportunity, work equally on their strengths and weaknesses, mitigate threats, and actively pursue the next opportunity. This work ethic is found in every successful artist and should be a framework for success.

Being an artist, being a creator is about being brave. For me it's emotional. You have to be brave, you have to be willing to stand on that edge. There's this old staying, leap and the net will appear. I always tell my students, I'm leaping with you. I'm not asking you to leap alone. You gotta be willing to go there 100%. —Jeff Coffin, saxophonist/composer

---

This passion must also extend to your overarching attitude that there is no "Plan B." If you choose to pursue this artistic life, it must consume your soul and every fiber of your existence. What you do daily to develop and hone your artistic skills cannot be done halfheartedly or as a part-timer. You must be "all in." This doesn't mean you forsake putting food on your table or caring for your family, but it does mean that you have to execute a thoughtful plan that gets you from Point A to Point B. If that means working as a server, Lyft driver, or other job, so be it—as long as it is a *means to an end*, not "making due." At some point, you will know if it's time for Plan B. However, as long as you keep your goal of being a professional artist in the crosshairs of your professional mission, these are only means to an end.

Through your personal story, your SWOT analysis, and by developing an artistic mission statement, we are confident you are now on your path to becoming a successful Artist Entrepreneur.

3

Finding Your Creative Space

Within the arts we explore the margins, interpreting varying shades of issues and coloring outside the lines. Artists strive to view the world from a unique perspective, from viewpoints that interpret life and life's stories through their personal lens. Arts educators need to help students find their voice and creative edge now more than ever.

The notion of creative thinking extends well beyond the arts. It seems reasonable to think that the biggest challenges in the world today, such as climate change, health care costs, and sustainable energy and water, are going to require creative thinking (coupled with science and technology) to solve these issues. Let there be no doubt that the next generation of artistic accomplishment will also require creative genius.

There are dozens, if not hundreds, of immensely talented young performing artists who are capable of flawlessly performing the Arutiunian Trumpet Concerto, dancing *Swan Lake*, playing the lead in *Hamlet*, drawing a realistic still life, or improvising over "Billy's Bounce." They have impeccable technique, have mastered the standard repertoire, and are ready for a hard-earned and sustainable career in the arts.

However, the reality is that opportunities to forge a full-time career as a professional artist are small. In today's unrelentingly competitive arts environment, young artists have received extraordinary professional training and have perfected the requisite technical skills and are qualified, often overqualified, for most jobs that are available. The fact that many college graduates are underemployed is a stark reality that will be shaping the future of higher education over the next several decades. At the same time, there continues to be a steady supply of immensely talented college graduates looking for opportunities as artists. The inverted supply-and-demand curve of talented arts graduates competing for a shrinking job market is not new. In fact, to counteract these realities, many arts programs have proactively created new classes, developed student engagement opportunities, and revised their curricula. Arts schools have also steered students into alternative majors, including arts administration, arts industry studies, music business, or theater arts. As a prime example of a new way of approaching arts education, a new program at Stanford University, titled "CS + x," allows students a dual degree in computer science and "x," any number of arts of humanities options. This innovative program allows students the opportunity to develop coding skills with a liberal arts education.

At Clemson University, we have adapted to this changing arts economy with our interdisciplinary Performing Arts degree. Students in music, theater, and audio technology progress together in a core curriculum that is supplemented by courses in Music Business, Arts Administration, and a collaborative capstone project. —Eric Lapin

At the same time, it seems clear that many creative, performing, and visual arts faculty in higher education have not changed their curriculum fast enough to face this "new normal" in the performing arts industry and, in fact, are partially to blame for the oversupply of highly talented and skilled graduates with few job choices. In fact, many schools have an abundance of fully endowed talent-based scholarships, grants-in-aid, and graduate assistantships. As a result, universities are on a never-ending treadmill that prepares students for arts careers that are no longer available. To feed this continuing cycle, faculty are pressured, and often evaluated (up to and including a tenure decision) on their success at filling their studios with high-quality students. This cycle is unrelenting, as are the extraordinary expectations and pressures for faculty to produce professional-level concerts, performances, and exhibitions.

I was at a university that had expectations and full-funding for instrumental studios (such as oboe and trombone) to fill the school wind ensemble and

orchestra rosters. Students were offered large scholarships to major in music and participate in the student ensembles. Faculty were under intense pressure to recruit and fill their studios with high performing students each year with reappointment and/or tenure often hanging in the balance. —Rick Goodstein

While the traditional performance degree may be outdated, the good news is that the new arts economy does present opportunities for talented artists to find a fulfilling and successful career. However, higher education in general needs to reevaluate its effectiveness in preparing arts students. In today's world of YouTube, file sharing, live streaming, and other new social and emerging media, academic training for performing artists has to be reimagined. Relevant classes in creativity, entrepreneurship, business, and relevant career preparation are needed for students to develop a career in today's arts landscape. A curriculum that helps students think creatively in order to discover and present unique and distinctive outlets for their art is crucial.

Specifically, formalized classes that give students new ways to approach their art such as multimedia presentations, digital technologies, collaborative interdisciplinary projects, and big ideas are crucial.

There is no doubt that these facts suggest that curricular change is mandated to address the new normal of today's arts landscape. In many cases, faculty have become stuck in an outmoded educational model that is tradition-bound and structured in a way they are familiar with. Leadership for these necessary changes can come from many sources, but must include a vision for change, one of the most difficult tasks in higher education reform. We have no doubt that a sea change must transform arts education or we will look in the rearview mirror in the not too distant future and ask ourselves what happened to our arts world.

As we articulated earlier, a career in the arts takes extraordinary grit, drive, and determination to overcome obstacles that will stand in the way of realizing a student's dreams. Unless you are a million-to-one prodigy, or the recipient of blind luck, there is no magic formula for success. You must be fully aware that there are numerous challenges and pitfalls in front of you, but a successful and fulfilling career in the arts can be a reality, despite the numerous obstacles today's students face.

These obstacles can be overcome, and those artists who persevere and doggedly push through these obstacles, overcome rejection, frustration, and lack of progress through hard work and determination are the most likely to succeed. While it is easy to get discouraged and think about altering course, the key to success is a PASSIONATE CREATIVE DRIVE.

As artists, we are trained to be creative. After years of endless scales and etudes, development of fundamental skills, a deep dive into the standard repertoire, scene development, repetitive rehearsals, and plenty of time at the "woodshed," we are expected to perform flawlessly, without any missed partials, squeaks, technical errors, forgotten lines, or missteps.

This expectation of perfection for performing artists is similar to the medical professions, engineering, or accounting, but at the same time, an anomaly for many other professions. In professional sports for example, Michael Jordan is known as one of the greatest basketball players of all time. He was one of the best clutch shooters in history, led the NBA in scoring for ten seasons, and is remembered for taking twenty-five game-winning shots. He also missed over 9,000 shots in his lifetime. In Major League Baseball, a batter will likely be an All-Star by getting one hit out of every three times at the plate, a 33 percent success rate. In sales, many professionals would be thrilled with a 50 percent success rate.

On the other hand, musicians are expected to be flawless 100 percent of the time. Nobody wants to hear a performance where two out of three notes are missed, the scenery falls down, dancers collide, or more notes are out of tune than in tune. Forgotten lines during a theatrical performance or a lack of fundamental footwork on the dance stage will not be tolerated. The same perfection is also mandated in medicine, civil engineering, or financial reporting. For artists, technical perfection is expected. Artists need to have mastered the subtle nuances of our art such as phrasing, dynamics, and interpretative expression, as these are all part of the creative spirit of performance.

If you want to be a professional musician, being able to play your tail off is a given, everybody can play. If you're going to be a doctor, you better be able to doctor. If you're an electrician, you better know about electricity. So being able to play, that's where it starts. Your ability as a musician may get you hired the first time. How do you get hired the second time? And the third time and fourth time? This is through relationships. If you show up late, if you show up unprepared, if you're a jerk to somebody, if you're not helpful, if you're not a team player, then chances are that they're going to call somebody else next time. If you are a great player and you are not working, it doesn't have anything to do with your musicianship.—Jeff Coffin, saxophonist/composer

Consequently, assuming that the technical aspects of our art are perfected, with so many talented artists wanting to build a sustainable arts career, students must look for ways to distinguish themselves. Fresh perspectives, new approaches, and a distinctive voice are needed, in addition to perseverance and a positive attitude. Unfortunately, raw talent is not enough and aspiring professionals must look for a creative approach to get noticed and develop a career.

CREATIVE THINKING

Wynton Marsalis has often referred to jazz music being the greatest example of democracy. We agree! At various points within the performance each band member must defer to another member of the ensemble. Everyone's voice is important and warrants being heard. The notion of improvisation demands that kind of deference. The same is true while working (or playing) with others. Painting, creative writing, and all the creative arts employ some type of improvisational/creative process.

The importance of creativity in this "new normal" cannot be overstated. As artists, it is assumed we are creative; however, thinking about creativity on a much broader scale must augment talent alone.

The value of creative thinking is being increasingly appreciated in today's evolving economy outside of the arts. The notion of solving old problems in new ways, the hyper-development of technology, and the twenty-first-century thought-based economy places a premium on creative thinking. Non-arts employers and businesses, both large and small, increasingly understand that creativity is a critically important trait to identify, develop, and promote in their organizations.

For example, a 2010 IBM survey of more than 1,500 CEOs from sixty countries and thirty-three worldwide industries indicated that the number one criteria for organizational success is creative employees, topping such personal traits as vision, rigor, or managerial skills. IBM stated that in order to navigate a highly volatile, increasingly complex environment, instilling creativity throughout the organization was a top priority.

This bodes well for students with a creative mindset, as the next generation of college graduates will find themselves in a world that is changing at an exponential rate, especially in the evolution of technology and the creative economy.

A new arts curriculum is needed that is refocused to develop creativity that will help prepare students not only for a sustainable arts career, but also for a future where jobs and technologies aren't yet invented. It is also interesting to note that according to the Bureau of Labor Statistics, the top ten in-demand jobs in 2010 did not even exist in 2004. Such skills as app development and video-based presentations are becoming increasingly important throughout the economy and artists have a tremendous opportunity to launch and build careers through a myriad of exciting emerging technology platforms. History informs us that these opportunities will continue to increase exponentially.

Google, which was launched in 1992 as a search engine at Stanford, now processes an average of 40,000 search queries *every second* (which translates to more than 3.5 billion searches per day and 1.2 trillion searches per year)! Think about how we found information prior to 1992 and imagine what the future might look like. Google is now working on a supercomputer whose processing power will dwarf the collective power of today's most powerful computers. How can aspiring artists fit into this new world?

Without doubt, having a creative mindset to attack the future and forge a sustainable career will serve students well. Students who can think "outside the box" in order to find creative solutions to current and emerging issues will have excellent opportunities both in and outside of the arts.

It's up to us to find creative ways of being creative. And so that's a lot of times how I'm looking at things. Right now I'm in the middle of something that involves a 40 piece choir, we had a 6 person dance troupe, we had a full rhythm section, my wife playing harmonium on some stuff and chanting, we had a marimbest, we had another flute, I was playing all the woodwind and saxophones, we had a Rabbi, we had an African-American woman who's a spoken word poet, who literally brings me to tears every time I hear her do her thing.—Jeff Coffin, saxophonist/composer

---

Former Secretary of Education Richard Riley foreshadowed this trend during the Clinton administration by asserting that, "We are currently preparing students for jobs that don't yet exist . . . using technologies that haven't yet been invented . . . in order to solve problems we don't even know are problems yet." With technology information doubling every two years, what a great opportunity to advance arts education if we can further develop and enhance creativity in every student.

DO YOU HAVE A STORY TO TELL? IF SO, WILL ANYONE CARE?

For aspiring performing artists, it is important to understand that the arts create opportunities to reflect on life and interpret the world around us. Successful artists help us understand the world in ways that shed insights, emotions, and nuances that can create joy, sorrow, happiness, or communicate despair. Great art tells stories through musical notes, colors, physical movement, words, emotion, dynamics. The fact that art can do this through the relatively simple vibration of airwaves, paint on a canvas, or the telling of a story is one of the true joys of life.

Despite the magic in the creation of art, the question remains: how do we find the creative edge that distinguishes ourselves and consequently gives us a distinctive advantage to "make it" and how does a degree in the arts pave the way to success considering today's realities. Make no doubt; it takes time, focused energy, a passionate drive, and unrelenting determination. There is no substitute for hard work. There will be pitfalls, failures, and setbacks—this is to be expected. Regardless, it is your determined spirit that needs to persevere.

How can you find that creative spark? There is no magic pill, and enhancing your creativity is a job. So you have to attack that job as a job.

In today's world of full-time digital connectivity, cellphones, and social media, developing creativity actually takes time to develop by simply sitting still, dreaming, and letting your mind wander. In our world of 24/7 multimedia inputs and distractions, we have lost the time and ability to be still and eliminate external inputs in order to focus your thinking on your craft, your imagination, and creativity.

A popular notion is that human beings have an uncanny ability to multitask. We study for an exam while music plays through ear buds, our cell phones are connected to multiple social media feeds buzzing, our laptops are open, and the television is tuned to *SportsCenter* or the *Real Housewives of Beverly Hills*. What an amazing ability we've developed to multi-task!

Or have we?

There is convincing research that indicates humans actually cannot multitask. According to neuroscientist Earl Miller at MIT, "People can't multitask very well, and when people say they can, they're deluding themselves." Our brains are simply switching from task to task with extraordinary speed. It's no wonder we have a hard time processing complex problems and creating time to think with multiple simultaneous distractions. For some people, having background "noise" is a prerequisite for concentration; however, developing complex ideas requires unrelenting single-mindedness.

Quiet Time

Simply taking time to sit still, dream, and focus in order to let your imagination roam is one of the most important steps in developing your creativity, what some have called "Blue Sky time." As a quote mistakenly attributed to Walt Disney stated, "If you can dream it, you can do it." We can't overemphasize the importance of being quiet—to get your mind into a creative space. To use your imagination, you have to give your brain time to work!

> **Exercise 3.1:** Try sitting still, without any external distractions, for fifteen minutes (preferably in a darkened room), focusing on a project you'd like to pursue. Take time, eliminate all distractions (including your phone!), and afterward write down your thoughts. It doesn't need to be a long narrative, just a few bullet points of your most significant thoughts during this time of reflection.

We spend a lot of time on airplanes and find that this is one of the best "quiet (or blue sky) times" we have—away from email, the phone, and normal distractions of day-to-day life. This book, and many of our best ideas, have come out of the anonymous world of an airplane seat.—Rick Goodstein and Ron McCurdy

You'll likely find that the fifteen minutes seems like an eternity. That is one indication that our attention spans are limited and we have been programmed to accept multiple simultaneous inputs, limiting our ability to develop our thoughts. Making time to let your imagination and creativity flourish is a crucial aspect of developing a creative mindset.

Experienced artists, performers, and athletes talk about their best work being done when they are in the previously mentioned "flow mode" and how this resultant focused energy yields extraordinary results. Giving yourself time to get into a flow state is a crucial aspect of the creative process, not just in actually making music, but in developing the mindset to be creative.

Another helpful tool is a journal of your best creative ideas. This organic creativity journal can contain anything that comes to your mind. You can think of this as a "flow journal." Keep the journal in your pocket or by your bed and write down your dreams, hopes, fears, and aspirations. Let your ideas evolve organically and, through a stream of consciousness, go down any rabbit trails your mind takes you. This journal can become a blueprint for your next creative project or job, or help you find your creative voice. You can use your phone to dictate short bursts of ideas as they occur and then take time later to transfer your thoughts to your journal. More than one creative spark of genius has been "discovered" in the middle of the night and forgotten.

Exercise 3.2: Start an organic creativity journal.

CREATIVITY AND LEARNING TO FAIL

Don't be discouraged by failure. All of us are taught, from kindergarten onward, that there are right and wrong answers and failure is not an option. Beginning with our first coloring books, we are urged to "draw within the lines." This is reinforced throughout K–12 education and is coupled with an unprecedented focus on standardized test preparation, school rankings, and college preparation. There is little doubt that most schools devote little to no time during the school day to let students develop creativity. While perhaps the Montessori, Reggio Emilia, and Waldorf educational approaches value creativity more than most schools, the development of creativity has largely not been a focus of K–12 education.

With so much time of the school day devoted to test preparation, many schools have reduced or even eliminated arts activities. This is a problem that is compounded by extraordinarily tight school budgets that don't prioritize arts and creativity. With decreasing school budgets and mandated curricula being imposed on public education systems by state and federal agencies, arts education is often the first discipline to be cut and never reappear.

Students (and parents) are also partially to blame as they strive for the perfect test score and often approach school from a "what is going to be on the test" mentality. With an overemphasis on standardized test scores, AP exams and various metrics associated with the college admissions process, arts classes are often left behind for "core" classes that are thought to directly affect and influence college admission consideration and/or scholarship opportunities.

We as arts educators are also often to blame for not helping develop student creativity as there is often an overarching priority for preparing students for their the next performance, concert, or exhibition, or winning the next contest or state festival while overlooking the development of student artistry and creativity.

I was shocked as a young college band director that many of my students had gone through marching "season" working on only three pieces of music. The entire focus of the fall semester was on upcoming contests, both regional and state. The scenario was repeated in the spring as the concert band focused on similar "successes" as determined by contest and festival results. —Rick Goodstein

I have known many jazz directors to begin preparing their "contest" selections in August for the big jazz festival in April! In many ways, this is the musical example of teaching for the test. For nearly nine months, these same charts are rehearsed and rehearsed again until they are flawless. Imagine the boredom! All of this is done to enhance the ensemble's chances of "winning." —Ron McCurdy

As a clarinet teacher, I often see middle and high school students who have prepared their scales for their county, region, and state auditions. The problem is, they haven't learned why they needed those scales. So knowing the scales the way they do is of no help in learning new music or improvising. This process doesn't teach them creativity or artistry. —Eric Lapin

CREATIVE COLLABORATORS

As artists, we live in a world of collaboration. Our performances are shared experiences, with both our on-stage colleagues and an audience. Although we may be a "business of one," our art does not live in a vacuum. The creative process can be enhanced through a collaborative effort, a working team of creative professionals. The collective energy of collaborative thinking is a powerful tool in developing creative projects.

Purposefully working as a creative team will allow you to bounce ideas off of others and let your project evolve. Talk to your friends, family, and teachers to flesh out your ideas. See if you can sharpen your thinking through a collaborative process into a concise narrative that focuses your thoughts. In short, don't hesitate to ask for input and refine your ideas.

As Walt Disney said, "You can design and create, and build the most wonderful place in the world. But it takes people to make the dream a reality." The value of collaborative thinking cannot be underestimated.

In both corporate and academic settings (and especially film and theater), collaborative, creative think tanks are invaluable. A room full of creative, driven professionals who are willing to bring their own creative ideas to the table can yield amazing results. For example, at mega-successful Nike, it's called the "Kitchen," Lin-Manuel Miranda calls his creative team the "Cabinet," MIT's Media Lab has spawned numerous disruptive innovations, Lockheed's Skunk Works has a long history of innovation as has Stanford's d.school. Coca-Cola's corporate spaces feature dozens of "huddle" rooms. These systematic creative collaborations yield creative results at an exponential level and provide a systematic method by which creativity can be explored collectively.

As people would move to town (Nashville, TN), I'd just kind of draw them in and gather them. —Jeff Coffin, saxophonist/composer

One of the most effective collaborative/creative idea generators is the "what if" or table-talk exercise. The process begins with an idea, big or small, and a selected group of collaborators. The facilitator presents the project idea and then opens the conversation with "what if we . . ." and then lets the collective creativity flow. Through this process, ideas will evolve, morph, and develop into several possible options for a project. As the facilitator, you keep the ideas flowing until the steam runs out or ideas begin repeating themselves. You will be amazed at the power of collaborative thinking and group creativity.

Exercise 3.3: Gather your "Cabinet" and facilitate a table-talk exercise.

Another successful strategy is to let some time pass or to "sleep on it" and let your creative ideas ferment. There is some research that suggests that your brain processes ideas after a period of time, overnight, and even over multiple days. What once seemed like a great idea can morph into something better or more nuanced, and conversely, what once seemed like a brilliant idea can all of a sudden feel like a really bad idea.

It's important to note that creative artists need to create a "safe" place for ideas to develop. During the creative process, you and your collaborators should not be hindered by what might be considered as a bad idea and every collaborator should feel as if every stakeholder has an equal and important voice at this stage of the process. Bad ideas, especially through a "what if" exercise, can evolve into something useful. The primary goal is to start with something—anything.

For an example of the "what if" process, and the creative world of Pixar films, read Ed Catmull's Creativity Inc.: Overcoming Unseen Forces That Stand in the Way of True Inspiration.—Rick Goodstein

---

The creative process takes time to develop and has been beautifully detailed by Peter Rummell, a legendary real estate developer and entertainment executive. He articulates six steps in the creative process:

1. The Inspiration

    This is the initial stage where being still, visioning, and personal interests come into play. Look at similar projects to yours; good and bad examples of what you are proposing; and failures. Creativity needs time to mature, much like a great wine. You can't force creativity—time, focus, and collaborative thinking will help encourage "outside the box" ideas. You will have some missteps, but you shouldn't throw anything away. This is the incubation period and when you should keep asking "what if . . ." Utilize your earlier vision/mission statement for a reference point so as to not lose focus.

2. Red Light/Green Light

    The frustrations of good ideas vs. bad ideas can take you down rabbit trails that might lead nowhere. Keep going—when you have ideas you like, take action and move forward with the ideas that resonate with you.

3. Home

    This is the point of reference you return to when your rabbit trails lead to nothing and you get lost in the maze of good and bad ideas. Refer back to your vision/mission statement. How far have you ventured off course? Go back home—what Rummell's calls "True North."

4. Agony, doubt, and panic

These crippling thoughts will come. It is true in every project, no matter how large or small. Even in multimillion-dollar film projects, with seasoned professionals at the top of their game, there are many moments of panic such as "how can we be so far over budget" or "what were we thinking" moments.

5. Laugh and Joy

Through all of the above, a sense of humor will make the process fun, or at least tolerable. Successful artists love what they do. Remember, this isn't brain surgery; there should be a sense of play and fun. If there is one thing that trumps everything else, it's a positive attitude.

6. It will be messy

The creative process never has a right or wrong answer. It isn't simple math. It's complicated, time consuming, and messy. Embrace the mess!

Conceptualizing, visualizing, and detailing your creative project is a crucial part of the process. As you begin to formulate your plan, begin making notes (recall the *Organic Creativity Journal*). Write everything down, no matter how small the detail. Just making notes and bullet points will help you refine your thinking. Outlines, a diary, and sketches are good means to keep a record of the evolution of your project.

At the time of publication, my personal journal of conversations, notes, ideas, and questions has filled up multiple legal pads. Keeping these ideas was definitely messy, but really helped organize our thoughts and keep the project moving forward.—Eric Lapin

---

While I am not a journal writer, I am an obsessive list maker and have a "notes" section on my iPhone that is filled with ideas, to-do lists, and reminders.—Rick Goodstein

---

Ed Catmull wrote, "Craft is what we are expected to know, art is the unknown." It is important to remember that failure is often part of the creative process.

Let the creativity flow!

4

It's Not about the Money— Yet!

One challenge artists face today is how to parlay their artistic endeavors into commercial success. In other words, how can artists make a living with their art? We do not subscribe to the "starving artist" mentality. Being a professional artist is just like any other profession where wages should be expected for services provided. However, for some reason there is a perception that artists are mostly happy-go-lucky creatures who are perfectly fine with offering their services for free, a box lunch, or for very low wages. This belies the thousands of hours devoted to practice, theory, and artistic intellect. In addition, it mistakenly attributes talent as merely a gift, something than can be given away.

I recall during my early artist years playing many receptions and other social events. The hosts would often say, "We can't pay you anything, but you're welcome to have all the punch and cookies you'd like." My response would be, "Would you offer to pay your doctor, or even your gardener, punch and cookies in exchange for their services?"—Ron McCurdy

---

I can remember in college once playing for a hot dog and a Coke at a local ice hockey game. All of my hours of practice, and my value for the performance that evening could be measured in hot dogs!—Eric Lapin

---

Sadly, this is the mentality that is often perceived about artists. This is especially true for those artists who are less established. We are "playing," therefore, we are not actually "working." During an artist's early development, when not yet at a professional level, it is often assumed you do not warrant a salary. The logical question becomes, "How do you know when you are considered a professional that warrants compensation for your services?" That is a question artists must answer for themselves. We believe that when the requests for your talents are in demand, you should consider yourself worthy of pay, regardless of whether you have yet achieved, in your mind, professional excellence.

My first gig was at the Elk's Lodge, I was 14! I don't remember what it paid, maybe $50. But it was enough for me to realize that I could actually make a living playing music.—Kenny Barron, jazz pianist

In this chapter, we address periods in an artist's life when money is not (and should not be) an issue or concern. By the time the decision is made to major in an arts discipline, aspirations of becoming a professional should already exist. However, even in college, the goal should not merely be about making money. This is the time when the developing artist should be honing their skills to become a professional.

But if you don't keep working hard—if you don't keep fully giving 100 percent—If you don't keep being fully present for your life, and that means onstage, offstage in your art, out of your art, in your life, then you're going to miss something.—Michael McElroy, actor

Money should not be the "be all, end all" at this juncture. You are strictly engaged in your art as an amateur, and your engagement is purely for the love of the art with an eye toward becoming a professional.

Across the country, there are non-professional choirs, galleries, performance spaces, community theatres, orchestras, and those who enjoy participating in the visual arts just for fun and intrinsic enjoyment. Typically, participating artists have other jobs that allow them the free time to engage in these kinds of extra artistic endeavors and spare them the stress of earning a living as an artist. We want to focus on what happens when an emerging artist aspires to become a professional artist. What kind of behavior should aspiring artists embrace if they strive to become professionals? How do you know if you have what it takes to make it as an artist?

Unfortunately, there is no one-size-fits-all answer to any of these questions. The one and only commonality is time. All who achieve a high degree of artistic success have invested a tremendous amount of time refining their skills regardless of the level of talent they arrived with on this planet. Ultimately, we cannot measure or predict who will have the desire to stick and stay. In short, there are no guarantees.

As a life-time music educator, I am amazed by my inability to consistently predict which students will "rise to the top" in the professional world. In some cases, students who I felt were marginally talented or could never "make it" have quickly forged a vibrant career, and others, who I would have bet on, struggle to find a solid career path in the arts. In many cases, it's simply being in the right place at the right time, and others, it's pure, simple luck.—Rick Goodstein

---

Over my 30-plus years of teaching, I have seen first-year students enter college with seemingly boundless talent and potential. In some cases, I have seen some of those students stagnate in musical achievement. Conversely, I have seen students who barely achieved admission into the university excel beyond my wildest imagination.—Ron McCurdy

---

PRE-COLLEGE YEARS

During a person's first exposure to art (which typically occurs when a person is in middle or high school), the furthest thing from their mind is, "How am I going to make a living with my craft?" Playing in the high school band, singing in the choir, acting in the school play, or drawing and painting is just plain fun! No one at thirteen is thinking about making a living. Unfortunately, that same mindset continues for many who decide to pursue the arts as a major in college. Students find themselves under the tutelage of a teacher who guides the direction of an artistic endeavor. Still at this level, most students are generally not too eager to think about life after college. They dutifully participate in school ensembles, rehearse, prepare for recitals, and address their other academic classes, and, before you know it, four years have elapsed. Then reality kicks in, and the student wonders, "How do I actually launch a career as an artist?"

I have seen the concerned look parents have when their child announces they want to major in music, pursue a career in dance, or become a play-wright. They know that their child is about to pursue a career where there are no guarantees. I have had several parents nervously ask me, "Dr. Mc-Curdy, when my child finishes his degree in music, will they have to move back home?" My response is, "I'd hold off on converting that bedroom into an office just yet!" I further elaborate by stating that students don't choose to become artists. Art chooses them! I often get a very puzzled look from parents when I make that statement.—Ron McCurdy

We all have examples where a student comes to school to study pre-med, business or another major and change into an arts major. These students became convinced that they needed to follow their heart and passion and change into an arts major. In every case, these students have overcome their own fears (and those of their parents), and become successful artists because of their passion, drive, and determination to pursue art despite the long odds.—Rick Goodstein

Once you are "called" to be an artist, you don't have a choice. Your laser-focused passion to be an artist should be the first thing you think about when you wake in the morning and the last thing you think about before going to bed. Mark Twain said it best, "The two most important times in a person's life are the day they are born and the day they figure out *why* they were born!"

PURSUING A CAREER IN THE ARTS

When students first arrive at the university to study their art, *Day One*, is when to start thinking of themselves as a small business. However, the small business should not yet be concerned about making money. Rather, it should focus on improving their artistic skills and learning how money is made in the artistic landscape. We caution them not to delay this kind of thinking until they are nearing graduation. Four years of college will zoom by in the blink of an eye, and waiting until graduation to focus on entrepreneurial thinking isn't an option. For music majors, in addition to participating in the school's music ensembles, each student should participate in and lead their own ensemble, whether it be classical, rock, folk, country, or a funk band. This will allow you to develop their skills as a professional musician. For theater artists, you should be involved in as many productions as possible, both on and offstage. You can learn as much from being on the property crew or a lighting designer as you can serving as the lead. As a visual artist, take every opportunity to expose your art in as many venues as possible. There is always someone who needs art in their lives.

When my son first entered USC as an eighteen-year-old freshman, I made the statement: "It's not about the money, yet! Your mother and I are taking care of your tuition, room, and board. All you need to do is focus on your studies and hone your skills as an artist." I suggested to my son (who is a trumpet player) that he form a trio consisting of a vocalist, pianist, and himself on trumpet. I also suggested that he contact some of his friends who were composition majors, and commission them to write for his ensemble, in addition to performing other standard classical literature. My other suggestion was for them to perform for anyone who would hire them. The goal was for them to be in perpetual "workshop" mode for at least two or three years while they polished their skills to become professionals. Finally, I suggested to them that while in school, his ensemble invest in building their promotional materials, that is, a quality video of performances, testimonials from presenters, website, and social media presence, etc. Again, I reiterated, "It's not about the money, yet!"—Ron McCurdy

---

There is a student, currently a freshman, who began busking on the streets in his spare time, formed a small, portable gigging band and self-created numerous opportunities to get paid to play. As he enters his second semester of college, he is able to pay many of his bills with ancillary income that was created from nothing but his talent.—Rick Goodstein

---

Most artists figure out why they were born sooner than many others. It is usually that little voice that offers encouragement and motivation to have the discipline to practice their artistic skills. However, that little voice can sometimes be like a "false prophet." What might appear to be motivation could actually be for reasons other than creating your art. It might be because a best friend is in band, theater, or your art class. You might have respect for a certain teacher or simply be influenced by the overall social climate of being around other artists. Being an artist is something you do because you "have" to do it, not because you want to do it. Either way, there should not be superficial reasons for choosing to be an artist.

"Do what you love, love what you do and share it with the world."

—*Gustavo Dudamel, Orchestra Director (LA Philharmonic)*

During the formative college years, the young artist is not saying, "I'm going to pursue the arts because this is going to make me rich and famous." Often when material things motivate a would-be artist, those careers are short-lived. If an artist is creating art with the intention of trying to figure out what the audience will "like," that modus operandi is similar to a dog chasing its tail.

I'M A FREELANCE ARTIST!

The advice I offered my son is the same advice I offer every freshman entering college. Sadly, my son did not heed my words of advice. He and so many students found it much easier to spend time in the school ensembles and not think about the kinds of things necessary to become a professional. My son graduated from USC In 2008 and has not been able to gain any traction as a professional artist. This is typical of so many students who simply do not (for a variety of reasons) figure out how to mount and sustain a career in the arts.—Ron McCurdy

Five years ago, I addressed my Jazz Pedagogy class to ask each student (all seniors) what was next in terms of their continued artistic journey. The response I received shocked me. "Well, I have a few gigs scheduled next month"; "I'm going to teach a few lessons, and then I'll just freelance." When I heard this, I listened with a very calm demeanor, however, on the inside, I was agonizing, "Are you kidding me? You (or your parents) just spent over $250K for you to receive an education from this very prestigious institution, and all you have to show is a few gigs next month and your desire to freelance?"—Ron McCurdy

In music, very often those artists who do freelance work are those who get calls from contractors to do theatrical pit orchestra gigs or television and movie recording work. These are typically highly skilled artists that have been a part of the work-for-hire music scene for many years that is controlled by a small number of powerful contractors. These musicians comprise a very small number of a select group of artists who do 95 percent of all of the recording, television, and film work in a given market. For the inexperienced young musician, this means your phone will not ring very often. Unfortunately, acting roles, gallery spots, and poetry readings are controlled in much the same way in this gig economy. We ask students who speak of engaging in freelance work, "Do you know Lance, the musician?" The student will almost always have a puzzled looked look on their face. Eventually, they are told that Lance is the musician whose skills are not quite at the professional level, so he ends up working for free. In other words, he's *Free-Lance*! The same mentality needs to be in focus for visual and theater artists. At some point, you need to stop giving away your art.

Artists must ask themselves, what are the ways in which we are taking ownership of our own artistic journey and artistic destiny?—Michael McElroy, actor

---

Unfortunately, this scenario continues to be repeated at colleges and universities every year. While some of this is due to a naïve understanding of the landscape of the arts profession by young artists, much is also attributed to the lack of preparation for careers in the arts many of our students receive while in college.

CREATIVE INTEGRITY

Creative integrity has to do with artists telling stories that speak to their artistic core values. What matters to you? What is your story? These are questions that artists must answer for themselves. Earlier in this book we suggested several specific methods to find your creative voice and discover your artistic DNA.

Creating art is personal and very much an individual endeavor. There is no better example than Duke Ellington, who was one of the greatest examples of an artist who understood the convergence of art and commerce. Ellington suggested that whenever art and commerce collided, more often than not, the art would be compromised. When artists engage in the creative process as discussed earlier, if they are thinking about crafting art that will be "liked" by the public, their art is immediately compromised. They will have sacrificed the creative integrity of their art. This is exactly what Ellington was referring to in his statement. We emphasize that artists are storytellers. They do not see the world in the same manner as non-artists. We will return to Ellington later in this book to give further examples of his genius as a true Artist Entrepreneur.

For example, when musicians or dancers hear the sounds of the subway train, they hear rhythms that might appear in a composition or choreography. When a visual artist is moved by a sunset, that becomes the subject of a painting or drawing. When thoroughly engaged in the creative process, the true artist is not thinking, "This is going to make me rich and famous!" They are bound to a form of storytelling. They are creating art with the highest degree of integrity and honesty. The best artistic creations are those that connect with some aspect of the human spirit. As Duke Ellington's career blossomed and his notoriety as a composer gained momentum in the 1930s, he began doing something other composers of his generation had never done. He composed music with each band member in mind. Instead of listing the instrument (i.e., Alto I, Trumpet II, or Trombone I, etc.), Ellington listed the names of each musician who played that particular part; so, the score would read Johnny (Hodges), Harry (Carney), and Juan (Tizol). Ellington knew the strengths and weaknesses of each band member, and by knowing the talents of his band, he was able to cultivate a sound that was uniquely "Ellington." Other professional bands have attempted to play Ellington scores, yet the results have never been authentic. They lack the same personality and creative integrity Ellington injected in his compositions.

Be authentic is whatever it is that you play. Retain who you are.—Jeff Coffin, saxophonist/composer

Similarly, Shakespeare wrote roles for specific actors in his company, The Lord Chamberlain's Men, based on their expertise. Richard Burbage, a member of the company, thought of as the greatest tragic actor of the day, played Hamlet, Othello, King Lear, and Macbeth in some of Shakespeare's greatest roles.

Another very important lesson we can glean from Duke Ellington is how to reinvent ourselves to stay current with the climate. America's musical taste began to shift with the advent of World War II, signaling the end of what was known as the Swing Era. By the end of World War II, Big Bands had already begun to wane, and America was starting to embrace rhythm & blues and rock & roll in the 1950s. This meant that fewer venues catered to

Big Band music and dancing which meant that bands had to figure ways to stay relevant. Several major bands, including Woody Herman, Harry James, Count Basie, and even the King of Swing, Benny Goodman, had to close shop for a while. Ellington's was the only notable band that was able to sustain itself during this transformational period, and it did so via royalties and self-commissions. Rather than follow the path of other artists who attempted to be popular, Ellington maintained his artistic integrity.

At the end of World War II, another style emerged known as Jump Swing, a comedic style that encouraged dancing and served as a forerunner to rhythm & blues. Several of the jazz musicians who leaped on the Jump Swing wagon found their careers short-lived, with the notable exception of Lionel Hampton. But as America's taste continued to evolve, Ellington wrote for television, movies, sacred music, and other long forms that were not generally associated with the jazz idiom. America may have stopped dancing to swing music, but Ellington simply found another path to remain true to his art. As an intellectual and Artist Entrepreneur, Ellington was able to understand the artistic climate and adjust his art to fit the changing landscape. As a result, his working band was together without interruption for fifty years!

I have tremendous respect for Lin-Manuel Miranda, who took an existing American Art form, the Broadway musical, and turned it on its head with "In the Heights" first and more recently with the smash hit, Hamilton. *Miranda has been able to incorporate rap, hip-hop, and contemporary dance into an art form that had become stale. The huge cross-cultural success of* Hamilton *through creative genius, Miranda has brought new audiences to musical theater and enjoyed commercial success beyond anyone's wildest dreams all while maintaining his creative integrity.*—Rick Goodstein

WORKING SMART, NOT HARD

While there is no substitute for hard work to launch a musical career, many artists "spin their wheels" in the process. Usually, those who tend to stumble are those artists who have not taken the time to study the situation and do the homework necessary to understand the musical landscape. "Working smart" certainly does not mean that there is some trick or gimmick to put you ahead of the class. It simply implies that you have taken the necessary steps to map out a game plan to define the vision for your artistic career. This vision should be a living and breathing idea, a fluid process. It should not be etched in stone as it may, and probably should, change along the way. Each artist should design, and regularly redesign, their own unique path.

Consequently, it is also incumbent on higher education to redesign curricula that will foster an artistic vision that goes beyond skill development, preparation for the next performance, recital, or exhibition and offer structured opportunities for developing students creativity and entrepreneurial thinking. But in the end, your career is your responsibility as an artist.

I once heard a pastor speak about the importance of maintaining a vision for one's life. Of course, he was speaking in religious terms, but the same concept is applicable to the vision one should have for an artistic career. The pastor stated, "Vision is like underwear. It should be yours, and it should be fresh!" Everyone in church laughed that day, but it struck me how apropos that advice is for an artist.—Ron McCurdy

---

TIME MANAGEMENT

For the artist, time management is crucial. This is especially true for those artists in the early stages of their careers. Emerging artists will often serve in a variety of roles to enhance their careers. Very often these young artists find themselves functioning as manager, agent, lighting designer, publicist, arranger, dramaturge, or even stagehand. Given the importance of each assignment, the artist will be more effective if their time is managed efficiently.

Our time management strategy that is especially geared to creative artists include the following practical recommendations:

1. Create a daily "things to do" list;
2. Invest at least 25 percent of your time on business matters;
3. Keep up-to-date on technology;
4. Avoid negativity and "glass half empty" thinking;
5. Embrace the process;
6. Visit museums, libraries, attend plays, concerts, and other cultural events;
7. Find time to remain connected with friends and family;
8. Keep your skills at the top of their game;
9. Eat healthy and exercise regularly.

There are many self-help calendars, time-management gurus, and online motivational tools. If you find yourself struggling with implementing a good time-management strategy, there are dozens of free and commercial programs available.

I know a professional artist who is an obsessive list maker/goal setter. He carries around a small notepad which contains daily, short-term, and long-term goals. He rewrites the list daily to remind him of his goals. I also have a son-in-law who has a list of goals laminated and pasted on his shower so he will see them every day as a motivator.—Rick Goodstein

---

Exercise 4.1: Put together your to-do list for advancing your goals.

BEING MOTIVATED AND RESILIENT

As in most endeavors in life (but especially in the arts), you will be told "no" far more times than you will be told "yes." The artist should understand that "no" should be thought of as "not right now." This must be the mindset, otherwise the constant "no's" will cause the artist to give up. In the earlier mentioned *Juilliard Effect* study, Wakin cites that only half of a particular Juilliard graduating class remained in music. There are several reasons for this dropout rate among extremely talented and gifted artists, but the one that most resonated with us was the fact that graduates had become disillusioned about the music profession.

There are numerous roadblocks that sometimes contribute to artists giving up on their dreams. Many artists give up because they lack the knowledge of how to navigate the artistic landscape. (We'll discuss this challenge in more detail in later chapters.) Another barrier is the inability to "stick and stay." Choosing the arts as a career is one that does not offer any guarantees. With the popularity of reality television shows like *America's Got Talent*, *The Voice*, or *So You Think You Can Dance*, success often seems to come overnight. Some artists seem to think that one day you're working at Pizza Hut (nothing against Pizza Hut) and the next day you have a lucrative recording contract with a major record label, been cast on Broadway, or offered a solo gallery showing. Unfortunately, that scenario is seldom one experienced by most artists. We have all heard the stories of the Beatles performing for years before near-empty venues for little to no money. We know about the Jackson 5 initially being rejected by Berry Gordy and Motown, and Della Reese being rejected by Duke Ellington. In the art world, such masters as Gaugin, Seurat, and van Gogh, and writers including Thoreau, Emily Dickinson, and Melville never found commercial success during their lifetimes. There are countless artists who have toiled for years, performing to near-empty rooms without compensation, before their big break occurred. The one universal theme for all of these groups or individuals is that they refused to quit or to take "no" for an answer. We emphasize, "no" means, "not right now!" This must be the mentality for every artist. Quitting is not an option!

In the 1940s and 1950s, it was common for most jazz musicians to have a "day" job to support their musical habit until their big break occurred. Today, parents often ask, "Shouldn't Johnny have another degree in education to fall back on just in case?" Our response is resolute: "I know this is not what you'd like to hear and maybe this is not the most practical approach to having a career in the arts, but, if you have something to fall back on, then you probably will." The moment the going gets rough, you will abandon your art. But you must learn to make it a business endeavor as well as an artistic one. We began this chapter talking about how your art is not about the money—yet. As you have seen, there are various strategies and foundational steps you can take to begin a sustainable career as an Artist Entrepreneur. As your career evolves, Artist Entrepreneurs are never starving artists, but purposely and intentionally thriving artists.

5

Choosing and Building Your Team

Choosing those with whom you will collaborate in an artistic expression is in many instances similar to choosing a partner. All the things you would expect in a personal relationship you should have as part of your team. Your team should be competent and highly skilled at their respective assignments and members who will have your best interest at heart. You want to have people you trust and enjoy their presence. You also want people who are performing at the highest artistic level. At times, you will spend more time with these individuals than you will with your own family. This is especially true when you begin to tour your art. Will you enjoy those moments when you're stuck at the airport because of flight delays or in long rehearsals?

WHO SHOULD BE ON YOUR TEAM?

First and foremost, you should think of yourself as a small business. Even though you think of yourself as an artist, as we've stated, in the twenty-first century you absolutely must be mindful and strategic on how you organize and balance your business and artistic life. The two must go hand in hand. Most artists would prefer if someone else handled all of the business items, but usually at some juncture you, the artist, will need to be responsible for handling all phases of your business. This is especially true in the early stages of your career. Having an agent, manager, and attorneys can be tricky. Managers and agents are also looking to get paid. Therefore, they tend to work only with established artists or those young artists that are rising stars. Even the rising star artist must demonstrate that they are worth the gamble. We mention this because the artistic life span of most artists is relatively short. It could range from five years to fifty, but the latter is rare. "One hit wonders," such as Vanilla Ice and the bands that recorded "Macarena" and "Who Let the Dogs Out," often find initial popular success but cannot forge a sustainable recording career. There will be a limited amount of time that you will be able to generate substantial income. Therefore, all of your endeavors should be done with an eye toward shaping your business. As you begin to assemble your team, it is imperative that you select individuals who possess a shared vision for your artistic endeavor. It also helps if there is good chemistry between you and your colleagues. If you're going to spend substantial time with these individuals, it helps if you get along. The saying "time is money" is very true. You should be in a mindset where you are making the most of every moment you have. This is not to say that you should not have a social life, but hangin' out with your friends should not become a way of life.

YOUR CREATIVE ARTISTIC TEAM

Most artistic endeavors involve some form of collaboration. Unless you are working as a solo artist (e.g., solo pianist, visual artist, etc.) you are often having to work with other artists. If you're the leader or visionary for the group, then your task is huge. In addition to articulating your vision for the artistic endeavor, you've got to convince your colleagues to "buy in" to your vision. What is the end goal? Can you answer the WIIFM question for your colleagues (What's in it for me?)? Why is this endeavor important? What kind of artistic statement are we trying to make? These are all important questions that will be asked and must be answered. These questions and answers will help you decide who should and should not be on your artistic team.

It's like you have to really think about what it is that I want to do and then surround yourself with people that are going to help you do that.—Michael McElroy, actor

---

The greatest gift my band has ever given me is the gift of collaboration. —Jeff Coffin, saxophonist/composer

---

SHARING YOUR VISION

As you begin to build your team, it is crucial that you articulate your vision for whatever enterprise you are about to embrace. One of the biggest mistakes many artists make is to not verbally share "why" we embarking upon this project. The goal should be to have everyone working and moving in the same direction. As you share your vision, that statement should include long term and short-term goals. The short-term goals may include the completion of a major project. An extension of those goals may include booking a certain amount of performances or exhibits. Is there a need for management? What size venues will be the best fit for your project? Is everyone's role well defined? These are but a few of the questions you will need to answer as you share your vision for your artistic endeavors when working with others. If you are the "leader" of your collaboration, it is important to include your colleagues in some of the decision-making process. Why is this important? By including your colleagues in this process, you help create an excellent group dynamic. The other members of the collaboration will develop a sense of ownership. They now have a reason to be "all in."

When Dabo Swinney became an improbable and unpopular choice to become Clemson University's head football coach in 2008, he sold his unapologetically enthusiastic vision of a thirty-eight-year-old interim head coach, who had never even been a coordinator, to one of college football's most respected head coaches by stating that his players were going to be "All In" using a reference to a gambling act. The "All In" brand exists to this day and is a staple of his program as Swinney has become one of the top football coaches in the country with four consecutive trips to the College Football Playoffs. — Rick Goodstein

It is our belief that no one will love your projects as much as you do. As leader, one of your tasks is to exude the kind of passion about your work that will be contagious among your colleagues. It's almost as if you are serving as a "cheerleader" for your project. Your authentic enthusiasm will become infectious.

When I was playing with Bela Fleck and the Flecktones, Bela told me to let us collaborate with you. Let us find our way around your music. It was stunning. What leader does that? None, nobody. It was an incredible lesson for me. — Jeff Coffin, saxophonist/composer

BUSINESS PARTNERS

There's a kind of "chicken or the egg" matter when it comes to having business partners. How do you obtain management if you have not done anything of major significance as of yet? Let's assume you have made significant strides as an artist and your career has gotten so busy you can no longer manage your own affairs. You have produced a series of recordings, had several major concerts, recitals, plays with favorable reviews. If you're a musician, you've got several decisions to make. Do you sign with a record label or publisher? If you're planning a six-month tour, how do you address the matter of contracts? These questions and many others are the kinds of issues that will require high-end professional assistance. At this stage, here are the primary business partners you'll need in order to maximize your earning potential.

PERSONAL MANAGER

This position is without question the most important person on your team. They can create an unlimited amount of success for an artist or they can wreck any chance you might have had of mounting and sustaining a career. The role of the personal manager is to oversee and assist with the direction of your career. This person will help shape all aspects of your career. This could include everything from your stage costumes to making decisions on tour schedules, and everything in between. Think of the personal manager as your Chief of Staff. It is always important to have an "out" clause in the contract with your manager. You should always hope for the best, but plan for the worst. Just as personal relationships can deteriorate, so can professional relationships. The breakdown in those relationships can occur for a variety of reasons (i.e., lack of artistic growth, dispute over commissions, philosophical differences, etc.). Managers will ask for what is known as a sunset clause. This is a clause designed to have your manager receiving part of your earnings for a designated period of time. These earnings are to allow for potential deals that were in the works at the time the relationship ended. The artist should (for obvious reasons) push for as short of a period for this sunset clause as possible.

Since identifying a manager is in many ways the same way you might choose a partner. There absolutely should be a certain level of trust knowing that your manager has your best interests at heart. I was fortunate to have found a manager who had seen my performance and offered to join my team. She offered tremendous guidance and helped to shape my artistic direction.—Ron McCurdy

You want to have someone who is a go-getter and someone who is not content to simply wait by the phone. The agent's main thing is booking gigs. The manager will also book some gigs, but they will also line up interviews, publicity, travel, itinerary, hotels, ground transportation, those kind of de-tails.—Kenny Barron, jazz pianist

COMMISSIONS

Typically, managers will receive a 15 percent to 20 percent commission from the gross. Artists who have established careers can sometimes negotiate a lesser commission. The 20 percent commission usually means a full service manager who is handling all aspects of the artist's career. If you are an artist with an ensemble with five or more members, and you're dividing the income equally, you can see how the 15 percent to 20 percent of the gross to the manager can really affect your bottom line. The commission from the gross is important because the artists are paid from the net, meaning they are paid af-ter expenses (i.e., travel, hotel, food, ground transportation, marketing, etc.). Once you do the math, it is easy to see that the manager could possibly make more than the ensemble members. This could easily cause friction between the ensemble and the manager. In recent years, there has been a softening of this kind of an arrangement due to the challenging arts economy and the extraordinarily thin margins. Some artists are able to agree to a 15 percent commission and in some rare instances, managers will accept their commis-sion from the net, meaning after expenses.

ATTORNEY

Any serious artist should not move forward with any legal arrangement without the assistance of an attorney. This is especially true when agreeing to signing recording contracts, tour dates, or any legal transaction that involves commerce. We are aware of the horror stories many artists have faced who were not aware of the intricacies of the business only to find themselves in a one-sided deal that did not serve them well. One only has to look at the infamous representation and 50 percent commission that Col. Tom Parker provided for Elvis Presley or the widely known misrepresentation that Jerry Heller provided N.W.A to understand the importance of solid legal representation and contracts. This is especially important to have legal counsel at the early stage of your career when a false move could have a long-term negative impact on your career development and financial security. Attorney fees can run from $250 to $850 for high-end lawyers. This sounds expensive, but it will make the difference in protecting your legal rights.

BUSINESS MANAGER

As you begin to tour and generate income, you will have a host of expenses including payroll, taxes, travel expenses, and basic handling of (hopefully) large sums of money. The business manager will oversee all aspects of your financial endeavors. As the artist, you should be aware of all transactions so that you know where your money is going. How many times have we seen an artist sue a personal manager for mishandling funds? Matthew Knowles (Beyonce's dad), Colonel Parker (Elvis's manager), Frank Weber (Billy Joel's manager), Allen Klein (Beatles), and Jerry Heller (N.W.A) are just a short sampling of managers and business partners who took advantage of their client's finances. It is sometimes very difficult to prevent unscrupulous managers from pilfering the coffers of unsuspecting artist. Every artist should be just as meticulous about their business affairs as their artistic growth. We must not forget, performance art is a business and unfortunately, everyone will not always have your best interest at heart. The more you know about the intricacies of the business, the better chance you'll have of avoiding litigious situations.

BOOKING AGENCY

The booking agent and the personal manager should work closely together. The booking agent's job is just that—to book gigs for you and your team. They should be constantly contacting presenters to arrange for as many dates as you are able to perform. Booking agents unlike personal managers can represent multiple clients. Their commission is usually 10 percent of the gross. The most important thing is to define the dimensions of the business relationship. Just as we discussed with the personal manager, there should also be an "out" clause in the agreement with the agent for the same reasons.

NETWORKING

Networking is an essential part of building your team when attempting to mount a project. One of the most effective ways to network is to remain curious about the artistic expressions of your peers. You should spend time as often as possible going out to observe shows presented by your peers and colleagues. Demonstrate humility by making sure you compliment (when appropriate) artists' work you have observed. Imagine what types of opportunities for collaborations might exist with some of your peers. If you have a relationship with various artists, make it a point to be curious about their current and upcoming projects. Ask more questions about their work than trying to impress others about your work. This is a basic tenet of life. Speak less and listen more!

You can make more friends in two months by becoming interested in other people then you can in two years trying to get other people interested in you!
—Martin Atkin

ATTITUDE

As your team is constructed and attempts are made to move artistic endeavors forward, your attitude has much to do with the amount of success you will experience. One artist comes to mind when you think of the power of a positive attitude. We are again speaking of Duke Ellington. Ellington was able to maintain his band for more than fifty years. This was during a time when America's musical taste had shifted over time, yet Ellington was able to keep the band together while still remaining artistically relevant. He was also able to maintain a high degree of loyalty. It was not uncommon for several members to remain in the band for twenty and sometimes thirty years. Both drummer Sonny Greer and saxophonist Johnny Hodges remained with the band for more than thirty years. Many other band members had more than two decades of service to the Ellington band. Why was this possible? Ellington was known as a fantastic communicator. He shared a clear vision for his band and made sure they were part of the master plan for success. In Ellington's compositions, he would often write the names of the person playing that particular part. Again, instead of writing on the score, *1st Alto Saxophone*, Ellington would write Johnny (Hodges).

Exercise 5.1: List and describe what each immediate member of your team brings to the project.

Exercise 5.2: Create a list of artists in your area that you have cultivated a relationship with.

Exercise 5.3: Define their projects and what possible collaborations exist.

Once you begin to monetize your art, you will need to surround yourself with trustworthy "teammates" who have *your* best interests in their work. While your team may initially be an agent or a collaborator, you will likely need to build onto your team as you realize your goals. Our advice, and cautionary tales, are to choose your teammates carefully and to trust, but verify, that they are working for *you*.

I'm always looking for opportunities to be around people who are talented so that we can find ways to work together. Collaboration is exciting. It's a way of being fed by other people and their artistry. So I'm always looking for opportunities. —Michael McElroy, actor

6

The Emerging Artist and Self-Management

I have just created an artistic masterpiece, now what? How do I find the right venue? Whom do I contact? How do I market this work of art? These are some of the many questions every artist who has self-produced a work of art must ask and answer! Unless you are an established artist and have a team of agents and managers working on your behalf, you'll need to be self-managed and serve as your own agent. This chapter is designed to offer a few strategies to help the emerging artist gain an understanding of how to navigate the artistic landscape. This is the side of the business rarely if ever addressed in school. Some enterprising students with a knack for business will pursue this very tedious aspect of being an artist. Most will not! It's simply too hard and requires skill sets often not found in young artists or nurtured by institutions of higher learning.

I have noticed that more artists are aware of the business side of the equation. Many have their own publishing companies and record labels. Many have their own recording studios.—Kenny Barron, jazz pianist

---

The delivery of artistic content, whether through digital content or live performance, continues to evolve. In the music world, from 78-rpm vinyl to CDs and digital downloads, the constantly evolving business model of music delivery is another obstacle for artists to understand. It's crucial that young musicians, aspiring to make a career as a solo artist or band member understand the importance of generating interest on the current "en vogue" services such as iTunes, Spotify, or Amazon Prime, or the next evolution of the digital services era.

Live performances is another opportunity for musicians to help build a sustainable Arts Entrepreneur careers. One important skill set is the ability to verbally connect with presenters, donors, and anyone else who might be in a position to assist with the business side of the equation. Many young artists are shy and introverted and don't have the "people skills" to speak fluently about their projects. They are quite comfortable with their respective artistic crafts, but usually have difficulty walking into a crowded room and feeling comfortable enough to introduce themselves to strangers or to take a one-on-one meeting with a potential patron. Fortunately, this is a skill that can (and must) be developed. You must become comfortable talking to others about your art. This is part of the process you may have begun to embrace while engaged in the planning of your storytelling. During your "table-talk" sessions discussed earlier, you bounce ideas off of friends, family, and colleagues. This was a very important step that allowed you to think out loud while creating your project. Now that the project is completed, the task now shifts to you being able to discuss what you've created in hopes of convincing others to support your creation. Your goal in speaking to presenters, club owners, and patrons is to get them just as excited about your work as you are. In many cases, they will be the ones who will be in a financial or decision-making position to help move your project forward.

MANAGING YOUR OWN CAREER

Very few emerging artists will initially have external management as their careers begin to develop. There won't be anyone to guide the artist through the maze of the artistic landscape. There won't be anyone to contact presenters for bookings, craft and read contracts, handle financial matters, schedule tours, manage marketing and promotions, and so on. In other words, the artist will be responsible for all of these kinds of responsibilities. The artist will need to manage their own career.

I needed to develop this whole toolbox of skills on how to behave, how to respond to emails, how to book my travel, and all of those kinds of things. —Marina Lomazov, concert pianist

Assuming that you have created a compelling piece of art, the next task is to convince presenters that your creation is worthy of public consumption. The goal is also for you to receive compensation for your artistic endeavors. In essence, you are now required to be the spokesperson for your creative endeavors to convince those who are doing the programming that your project is worthy. Presenters have the task of creating a robust concert series, gallery showing, or theatrical performance to their patrons. Some are bolder than others. Some presenters will only book the well-known artist who will guarantee a full house, while some presenters will take a chance on lesser-known artist. We suspect you fall into that category; otherwise, you would not be reading this book! By your words and collateral materials, you will need to convince the presenter to give your art a chance. Think of your website as your business card. It will allow the presenter and your fans to peruse your artistry and to ascertain if your presentation would be a good fit for their venue.

THE STATE OF THE ARTS LANDSCAPE

As we've stated earlier, you should perceive of yourself as a business of one! The old jobs have mostly disappeared. The arts economy is constantly evolving and today's artists must change with the times. It is quite likely that by the time this book is published some of the concepts discussed could possibly be obsolete. Those born before 1970 will remember LPs, 45s, cassette tapes, eight-tracks, and record stores. iTunes, Pandora, Apple Music, Spotify, and a host of other formats have made these other models a thing of the past (even though vinyl is making a small comeback). Just as these formats for selling music have changed, the manner in which presenters are contacted has also changed. The days of sending hard copies of your press kit have long ended. No one will accept or have time to review your materials if you send a bulky press kit.

As a presenter for the Brooks Center for the Performing Arts, the days of hard copy press kits are definitely over. Video samples, website links, social media channels, and digital streaming options are so much easier on the people deciding whether or not to book your group. A bulky CD or VHS (yes, for real!) demonstrates to presenters that the artist is out of touch with the current arts landscape. We'll quickly move on to the next artist.—Eric Lapin

---

The delivery of artistic content, whether through digital content or live performance, and how artists monetize their art continues to evolve. From 78-rpm vinyl to CDs and digital downloads, the current business climate of streaming music services is another blow to the individual artist as young artists need to understand and market methods to generate interest and clicks on iTunes, Spotify, or Amazon. My experience tells me that the rate of technological evolution is unlikely to slow down and artists at every stage of their career need to pay attention to the shifting landscape.—Rick Goodstein

Presenters want to do one-stop shopping. That is, find all of your information, which includes musical examples, video, bios, photos, testimonials, technical rider, stage plot, and any other information that will help the presenter gain a better sense of what you are presenting. All of this information should be found on your website. Your site should be easy to navigate with all of the necessary and pertinent information listed to help the presenter learn more about your act. Your website should be an ever-evolving portal of information. We suggest updating your site at least every six months. You want to give enough time for the content to land without becoming stagnant. By simply regularly adding new content (i.e., testimonials, photos, new videos, any awards or honors, etc.), you will attract more traffic to your site.

Exercise 6.1: Begin to develop your website.

Another very crucial aspect of today's business is the inclusion of social media. This is a must! This is how you drive traffic to your website by posting information about your act on your social media pages. Use your Facebook page for good and not evil! Many artists use their Facebook page as an opportunity to offer some social or political rant, discuss their personal life, or to engage friends. While this is certainly one way to remain connected with "friends" it is not the way to promote your activities as an artist. No one cares what you had for lunch! We suggest using Facebook, Snapchat, Instagram, Twitter, LinkedIn, etc. to keep your fans informed. You should post on each of these formats at least two to three times each week. This will also vary depending on the platform and intended audience. Treat your postings as if you were casually telling your friends about your artistic endeavors. This will help your content come across as authentic and genuine. There's a thin line between informing and bragging or seemingly trying to sell something. The tone should be positive and genuine.

Exercise 6.2: Conduct an inventory of your social media presence and create appropriate new content to support your work.

We also know that many artists are bypassing record labels in today's market. They self-promote on their YouTube page by giving away music. Much of this model started with the 1990s Napster model of "if you can't beat 'em, join 'em." Many artists now give away their music in hopes of gaining an audience to purchase tickets to their "live" shows. There, the artist will also sell their merchandise as yet another source of income. In a very crowded field of great artists, how do you distinguish your talents from the thousands of other acts vying for the same gigs?

It is important that we look beyond talent, as Angela Beeching suggested. Remember that in the arts, we have supply-and-demand issue. We have more supplies than there is demand! As we've stated earlier, there is an abundance of talent all of whom are vying for the gigs and opportunities that exist. A host of artists who have written brilliant scores, plays, and scripts, and are gifted artists who for one reason or another can't seem to get past first base. This is where the task of thinking and behaving as an entrepreneur is absolutely imperative. Unless you immediately obtain an agent and management, you as the artist will need to assume those roles yourself in addition to remaining engaged on the creative activities. Unfortunately, this is the fate of 99 percent of most emerging artists.

WHAT IS A NICHE MARKET?

Defining your niche market is one of the most important first steps of being able to successfully market your creation. We live in a multicultural world where a variety of genres and styles are present and embraced. One of the challenges the artist will need to address is to define your market. In other words, who is most likely to enjoy and support my artistic creation? What venues tend to support the kind of art that I've created? What venues are supporting groups, ensembles, or visual arts that are similar to what I've created? What is the market for my poetry or screenplay? These are some of the questions that will need to be answered as you develop your strategy for moving forward. For example, if you have an avant-garde ensemble that involves multimedia, dance, and spoken word, chances are you should not approach a jazz club. Conversely, if your artistic presentation involves a string quartet playing the music of Beethoven, Brahms, Mozart, your venue of choice probably will not be a venue that routinely support ska bands. The examples seem quite obvious, but you'd be surprised at the lack of knowledge that many emerging artists display when it comes to knowing whom should they contact. The first step is to identify and visit the websites of ensembles that are similar to your ensemble. Look at their tour and concert schedule. See what venues are a part of their tour schedule. The next step is to gather the contact information for the artistic director or the person who is booking the venue. This information is golden! By contact information, I'm referring to their telephone number and email address.

Find out how often the venue books "live" music or schedules showings. Is there a chance for multiple night engagements or is it a one-off? Find out the booking season. Most major venues will schedule at least twelve to twenty-four months in advance. Clubs and school concerts tend to be on a much shorter booking window. For example, a college or university student activities board (usually student run) will operate at least one semester in advance (three or four months). Again, it is important to know the booking cycles of all of the venues you want to pursue. When possible, try to get a sense of what is the budget for any given venue. This can be tricky because fees vary from one artist to the next. As an emerging artist, it is more than likely your fee will be different from that of other more established artists in your field. It is helpful if you're able to speak with a business manager, agent, or mentor to have them help you with an asking fee for your services. As a visual artist, know what galleries show similar art, what exhibitions are coming up in which you can apply to display your art through TheArtGuide.com. For creative writers, know what publishers might be interested in your work and how to get the reviewers to look at your material.

It is difficult to negotiate on your own behalf. It isn't unusual that self-represented artists tend to low-ball themselves. They simply don't know how much they should ask, thus throwing out a number that is often below market value. Having done some homework becomes crucial if you are going to be self-managed. This will hopefully keep you from either asking for too much (thus pricing yourself out of the market) or low-balling your asking fee.

Exercise 6.3: Do your homework—research projects and presentations that appear to be similar to a path you envision for yourself.

ARE YOU A VISIONARY ENTREPRENEUR?

This is a term coined by Jeri Goldstein. Jeri has written extensively on the subject of Artist Entrepreneurship and has an ongoing blog to help emerging artists navigate the artistic landscape. The term "vision" infers that you have a sense of the direction your career is headed. You can envision what venues you will perform, the size and genre you will explore, and so forth. In short, you are imagining the scope of your career. This does not mean that you will be locked into a certain direction, but that you are offering some degree of structure or blueprint for the direction and aspirations of your artistic endeavors. The term "entrepreneur" suggests that you are willing to take a risk in actually doing something to move your vision forward. By combining these two words, *Visionary* and *Entrepreneur*, you are in effect taking on two distinctly separate roles. We'll discuss the role of the manager/agent in more detail in later chapters, but more than likely, this is a roll that most emerging artists must assume themselves. As the visionary and founder of your career, you are allowed to dream and hopefully dream big!

As my mentor David Baker once said, "you should be limited only by your imagination."—Ron McCurdy

The visionary will imagine all kinds of collaborative opportunities. They will develop the "right" team of colleagues to join their vision. The entrepreneur will have the knowledge to put those dreams and imagination into action. This will certainly involve contacting arts presenters, various venues, publishing companies. These are but a few of the characteristics of a skilled Artist Entrepreneur.

WHERE ARE THE VENUES?

As you were in the process of creating your "masterpiece," hopefully you could envision what venues are most compatible for what you've created. You've attended concerts, theatrical events, musicals, dance recitals, gallery showings, multimedia presentations to gain a sense of what type of venue might be a good fit for what you've created. While partaking of these artistic events, hopefully you have imagined your creation on stage or on display. You've looked at the size of the venue, the kind of clientele, the ticket prices, the caliber of artists who are part of the various series'. All of these variables help you to size up where you might fit at the moment. If you're a classical artist and you observe that Yo Yo Ma, Modori, Christopher Wool, or the Turtle Island String Quartet are part of the concert series or exhibition, and you're just launching your career, you might not be ready to be in that same league just yet; however understanding an artist's path can be extraordinarily helpful. You may need to find other venues that are still producing quality performances, but on maybe a lower scale. This doesn't make you any less of an artist, you simply need to wait your turn and continue to develop your craft. Sometimes it takes a long time to become an overnight success!

THE MAILING LIST

One of the most important items to begin developing is your mailing list. This is your lifeline and connection to presenters, club owners, and anyone producing artistic events. All that is needed is the name, position, phone number, and email address. If you have that information you're on your way! Now you have a place to start. Developing a mailing list is an ongoing process. Once you become a member of various presenting organizations, you will have access to a mailing list of their presenting affiliates (e.g., National Association of Campus Activities (NACA), Association for Performing Arts Professionals, (APAP), Arts Midwest, etc.). You can also do what we call prospecting for this information. For example, if multicultural affairs departments at colleges and universities are part of your niche market, then you can do Google searches to locate the necessary information. Or, if national and international jazz festivals are part of your target audience, you'll have the opportunity to gather this information from the May issue of *Downbeat* magazine. Each year, they list the dates, location, and contact information of the festival's artistic director. This information is golden! This is how you begin to collect this very important data.

The next step is where do you store this information? We suggest placing this information on an Excel spreadsheet. This is important because once you have accumulated over a thousand addresses, you'll want to send personalized emails to each prospective presenter. Mailer programs such as Constant Contact and Mailchimp allow you to upload all of your database thus allowing you to send personal emails all at once. One very important point is to try and personalize your correspondence as much as possible. Avoid sending emails to prospective clients with a "Dear Friend" greeting. There's a very good chance your email will never be read. The aforementioned email programs allow you to greet your prospective client with either their first name or with a handle and surname (e.g., Dear John or Dear Ms. Smith). We'll discuss this process in further detail later on.

Exercise 6.4: Learn the basics of Excel and start to build a contact list.

THE COLLEGE PERFORMING ARTS CENTERS

This college market is one of the appealing options for emerging and established artists. In addition to performing arts centers, student activities, multicultural affairs, and student inclusion offices all are engaged in varying degrees of programming a wide range of artistic presentations. Nearly every college or university will have some version of a performing arts series. The majority of these shows are booked as a result of showcases at regional or national conferences. These conferences include the Western Arts Alliance (WAA), National Association for Campus Activities (NACA), Arts Midwest, and probably the largest national conference for shows is Association of Performing Arts Professionals (APAP). The larger venues tend to book twelve to twenty-four months in advance. The smaller venues usually book within a year of the performance date. As an artist, it is necessary to make the investment to showcase at one or more of these conferences. There is a fee that can range from $1,200 to $2,000 for a thirty-minute showcase. This may seem counterintuitive for an artist to think in terms of paying to perform. It can become very expensive to showcase at one of these conferences, but if one show is booked, you will more than recoup your investment. You want to select your best compositions or the apex of your theatrical performance that you feel will make the best impression on prospective programmers. You should also have your two-minute elevator pitch of your presentation ready to go (more on this later). This might include why your presentation would be a "good fit" for any performance series. The more you can do to educate the programmers about your presentation, the better. Think of this as an audition. You are trying to convince the programmers that your presentation is artistically compelling and would be appealing to a wide demographic audience.

GETTING PRESENTERS TO ATTEND YOUR SHOWCASE

This can be tricky! By the second or third day of an arts conference, many presenters are burned out. They've been going to shows all day for two or three days straight and your showcase is on Day 4 of the conference. How do you get them to attend your performance? This is where having access to a manager or agent is crucial. Notice, we did not say representation, only access. Even if the agent or manager does not represent you, they will at times allow you to present in the room that they have rented for their clients and others. There is a fee you will pay to the agent for the opportunity. The agent will often have a booth at the conference as well. This is important because the agent will allow you to place your marketing materials at their booth. Plus in your emails to presenters, you'll be allowed to invite them to visit the booth, while alerting them of your showcase time and location. This allows for very good access to thousands of presenters. All you want is the chance to be seen by the presenter in hopes of receiving an invitation to perform at their venue.

The showcase experience can seem somewhat like a huge "cattle call." There are so many artists from practically every genre and discipline in the arts you could imagine. There are singers, dancers, jugglers, comedians, snake handlers, all kind of acts vying for the attention of the presenters. That experience alone can discourage you from ever wanting to showcase again. Usually, most groups are allowed roughly thirty minutes to offer a sample of their performance. Therefore, it's best to choose sections that will best demonstrate the depth and breadth of your performance. Avoid any long verbal explanations of your artistry.

We attend APAP every year looking for talent to book for the Brooks Center. When we attend a showcase, we are looking to hear/see your art, not hear you talk about it. With only thirty minutes to showcase, you are wasting time speaking. Presenters are going to book based on your art, not on your explanation of your art.—Eric Lapin

---

Action speaks louder than words. Perform as if you were in "Carnegie Hall" even though the room may only have a hand full of presenters. You never know who is listening. When possible, make it a point to introduce yourself to some of the presenters who attended your presentation.

LIBRARIES, MUSEUMS, AND CULTURAL CENTERS

This is yet another very good option in terms of presentation venues. Concerts and showings at these venues are often connected with a specific series of events or a thematic focus (i.e., Cinco De Mayo, Kwanzaa, National Poetry Month, Chinese New Year, Black History Month, etc.). As an artist, it is wise to sometimes build a show that will also have an educational focus. There might also be an opportunity to present a series of master class for student programs.

As a presenter for a theater on a college campus, we always look for music and theater events that also feature educational outreach opportunities. We want our presentations to connect with our audiences in as many ways as possible. For example, we look for opportunities for a jazz group to conduct a masterclass with our student jazz ensemble or for a theater company to conduct an improv or movement workshop with our students. This helps to develop a deeper relationship between the students and the artists.—Eric Lapin

---

I've attended the APAP Conference for years and have seen every type of showcase you can imagine. It never ceases to amaze me how agents can present unprepared or unpolished artists for presenters to consider booking.—Rick Goodstein

---

Exercise 6.5: Begin to plan educational outreach activities around your art.

What is important is to create a database with the contact information for programmers so that you or your agent can remain in contact with the venues. Much of this information can be found through state arts councils and their touring directories. In addition to learning about the venues, often you can find various funding opportunities. Applying to be part of the states touring directory also helps to establish your ensembles' credibility.

TELLING YOUR STORY?

When we speak of telling your story, we are referring to how you will convey what you have created to arts presenters, artistic directors, and club owners.

Unless you have a team of managers and agents working on your behalf, you as the young artist will need to be your best spokesperson for your creation. On several fronts, you'll need to be able to speak in a convincing fashion on why your artistic presentation is worthy of their time and investment. This same kind of storytelling about your creation is true if you are writing a grant proposal (more on this later) or speaking to a prospective patron. No one should be able to speak as passionately about your creation as you. This is a skill most did not inherit at birth. As mentioned earlier, many of us tend to be shy and rather introverted when it comes to speaking to large audiences, speaking in a one-on-one meeting or by telephone.

One of the first things we suggest is to write out your talking points. They should be very succinct and to the point as you articulate your "story." It should not be a memorized speech, rather, a series of talking points that will allow you to have a coherent conversation about what you have to offer as an artist. This will help you to organize your thoughts. Once you've crafted your talking points, read them (out loud) over and over until they sound natural and conversation-like. When possible, look for human connecting points (i.e., a mutual friend on staff or knowledge of a recent artists' performance at the venue in question, or some other personal connection). Before you attempt to speak with a presenter or patron, try your pitch out on friends, family, or anyone who will tell you the truth. Have them ask you questions about your project. Avoid speaking in slang or using the word "like" at the beginning of each sentence. This manner of speech will very quickly get you dismissed as someone who is clearly not professional and ready to function in a professional environment. The goal is to get the listener just as excited about your project as you are. Words and clarity matter!

> **Exercise 6.6**: The elevator pitch. Develop a forty-five-second "speech" that you could tell a complete stranger about your art and/or your project. Practice, practice, practice the elevator pitch until you feel 100% comfortable in your delivery.

KNOW YOUR VALUE

One point to keep in mind is the cost of your presentation. Every artist should have a budget for the cost of your presentation. One of the biggest mistakes by young artist is to lowball themselves when pitching their presentations to venues. In addition to the ensemble salaries, you must take into account a host of other expenses that will cut into your bottom-line. Most times travel will consume a huge part of your budget. Many venues will prefer to offer a contract that is all-inclusive, meaning there will be one check that will include ensemble fees, travel, hotel, ground transportation, food, and a host of other expenses. Ideally, strive for the kind of contract that will pay performance fees plus travel and hotel expenses. At times, certain venues will not be able to meet your budget. When that occurs, there may be other means of "horse-trading" to help move the deal forward. For example, maybe the venue will supply hotel rooms, ground transportation, and meals for the ensemble. Those kinds of negotiation can be a win-win for both the presenter and the artist.

Besides a single contract, some venues, and larger acts, insist on a base contract and a portion of the ticket sales. This type of contractual agreement is unusual for entry-level performers and typical venues; however, you should be aware of this type of contractual agreement.

ANCHOR DATES AND BLOCK BOOKING

Once you have booked an "anchor date," one of the most efficient ways to maximize your earning and artistic potential is to engage in block-booking. Let's say you have booked a concert at the University of Kansas. Once that date has been confirmed, take a look at the map at every possible venue within a 150-mile radius of Lawrence, Kansas. There's a very good chance you'll be able to book two or three additional performances while in the area. The obvious positive is that once you land in Kansas City, you can rent a car and drive to the additional performances without incurring the most expensive part of touring, airline expenses.

THE PHONE CALL

A huge part of your communication with presenters will take place via telephone calls. This too can be tricky, because you are not meeting in person and may not have the undivided attention of the listener. Also, phone calls are in some ways like social media, that is, the listener may not say things to you in person that they would over the phone. Additionally, you have to assume that the presenter is busy. In most cases, they were not expecting your call therefore it is possible that your call could be perceived as an intrusion on their time. In many cases your phone call to the presenter or venue will be a "cold call" and you will need to understand how this may be perceived by the presenter.

Many presenters (including this one!) prefer these phone conversations to be scheduled. We all have busy schedules in the arts with every second of our day booked, so having a scheduled call can help you gain more of the presenter's attention.—Eric Lapin

This is even more reason for having your pitch together so that you are not looked upon as wasting the presenter's time.

Here's an example of how a mock phone call might transpire:

MOCK PHONE CALL TO PROSPECTIVE PRESENTERS

Introduction

Artist: Good morning, my name is Randy Smith and I'm calling on behalf of the Music Performance Project. We are planning our tour schedule for the fall 2019 and spring 2020 concert season. If you are in the midst of planning your multicultural programs for next year, I would like to ask that you consider the Music Performance Project.

Information about the Project

Artist: The Music Performance Project is a multimedia presentation involving spoken word, jazz quartet, and videography that chronicle American jazz music.

Additional Opportunities

Artist: In an effort to engage the students, we have as a component of our presentation the Poetry Slam. This is an opportunity for the students on your campus to craft their own poems. Then the artist will compose original music to accompany the students while they open the concert for the Music Performance Project.

Further Opportunities

Artist: The Music Performance Project seems to work best when there is a linkage to some of the academic units. In addition to the concert, the artist can present masterclasses on a variety of topics throughout campus including poetry, composition, and arts entrepreneurship.

Fees

Artist: Our asking fee is $XXXX plus travel expenses. *(If the fee is beyond their budget, then ask if they have counterparts at other schools in the area that would allow us to block book in an effort to bring the fee down.) or (Is there a possibility to partner with some of the other academic units to help defray expenses? (e.g., music, English, American Studies, etc.)*

Follow-Up

Artist: May I send you additional information via email that will include a link to our website and other pertinent information that will further acquaint you with the Music Performance Project? After you've had a chance to review this material, please let me know the best time to follow-up with you.

Suggestions

Remember that the biggest challenge is to help the presenter distinguish the Music Performance Project from the hundreds of other projects presented to venues. For the Music Performance Project, the selling point is the cultural awareness the project offers.

It will absolutely require multiple communications with a presenter. They are busy with other things and we are usually not at the top of their daily agenda. There's a thin line between being persistent and being a nuisance! We want to find that spot that will allow us to remain on their radar screen without bothering them. We've found that an email first is best, then followed up with a phone call.

We also can't state the importance of being prepared for this call strongly enough. Make sure that you have information on fees, travel costs, other shows you're playing on the route, your technical requirements, and educational outreach materials at hand. No presenter (including this one) wants to wait while you try to pull up a document or rummage through your desk.
—Eric Lapin

Try to be as accommodating as possible. In short, the presenter is (most times) always right. Try and find opportunities to horse trade in an effort to book the date. If a school is not able to match the asking fee, then seek block-booking opportunities with nearby venues. Have the venue help recruit other venues or presenters to participate.

If you are unable to reach the presenter and must leave a message, it is important to speak slowly and clearly, leaving your name and phone number. As a courtesy, the phone number should be stated twice. This will give the presenter a chance to have pen and paper ready to write down your number. Your message may also state that you will follow up with both another phone call and an email.

Your greetings on your phone should also state your name and the name of your business. Try to avoid greetings that play long music excerpts before the greeting appears. I've heard examples of long distorted samples of music played for thirty seconds (which is an eternity for a busy person returning your call) only to have the voice stating, *"What Up, What Up, What Up! Can't come to the phone right now, so hit me up later. . . . Peace Out!"* All of your friends will think you are the coolest person on the planet (or not!), but the presenter will not share that same sentiment. That lack of professionalism will be apparent from the very beginning, thus running the risk of the presenter simply hanging up and not leaving a message. The goal is to give the appearance that you are a serious artist and understand the importance of comporting yourself as a professional.

NO MEANS, NOT NOW!

Booking your ensemble is in many ways a numbers game. By this, we mean, how many presenters do you contact in a given day, week, or month? If you are getting a 3 percent to 5 percent response from those you contact, you are doing well. If you make fifteen calls a day, you'll more than likely be told "no" on fourteen of those calls. The response we offer is "no" means not right now. Most times you'll be told "no" for a variety of reasons including not having the budget, not a good artistic fit for a given concert series, or can't agree on a date. Any of these reasons could be a deal-breaker and/or a delay.

7

Minding Your Own Business

Make no mistake, art is a business! From the moment it was discovered that there was an opportunity to garner a wage from artistic expressions, artists have had to figure out how to maximize their financial potential. Composers, thespians, painters, and dancers all had to figure out how to monetize their respective crafts. Each era has presented its own set of challenges. With each generation, the need for artists to better understand how to protect their intellectual property became even more crucial.

50/50 PARTNERSHIPS

We discussed earlier the importance of building your team. However, if you are the primary creator of your project, and you are bringing in partners, we do not recommend 50/50 partnerships. Just like a marriage, should things go "south" you might find yourself having to buy out your partner. If the project is your idea, then you should maintain the control and ownership of the enterprise. If you must bring in a partner, have them at a lesser percentage of the project, depending on their level of engagement. Regardless of the level of partnership, every collaboration should have a legal agreement in place. There are lawyers who specialize in entertainment/artistic law and a legal agreement outlining the dimensions of your business relationship with partners is imperative. This just might be the best $1,000 dollars you can spend as you launch your collaboration. There are countless law firms and lawyers that specialize in the arts. Organizations like the Volunteer Lawyers for the Arts in New York even provide reduced rate or pro-bono legal guidance and services.

PROTECTION OF INTELLECTUAL PROPERTY

The founding of the American Society of Composers, Authors and Publishers (ASCAP) in 1915 cemented the fact that artists would be paid for their intellectual property. It was a case settled by the Supreme Court to decide a case between Victor Herbert versus the Shanley Restaurant. Herbert insisted that he be paid a fee for one of his songs performed on a player-piano during dinner service. This landmark decision in 1917 made it possible for composers, musicians, writers, and authors to be compensated financially for their intellectual property. From that moment to this day, that has been the law of the land. In 1930, the European Society of Stage Actors and Composers (now SESAC) and in 1939, Broadcast Music, Inc. (BMI) were founded. While we won't go into a lengthy discussion detailing the differences between each organization, the important part is that every artist who engages in creating art should belong to one of these organizations in order to be paid for public performances of their art through stipulations in the United States copyright laws. For example, if you are a composer, imagine the royalty checks generated each year by the Gershwin, Mancini, or Michael Jackson estates. You want to have the gift that keeps on giving! There are many textbooks and web resources that will explain the copyright laws in detail and how to register your intellectual property. Donald S. Passman's book *All You Need to Know about the Music Business* is a great source for in-depth information regarding copyright laws.

8

Arts Leadership

For decades the study of leadership has been a popular topic in the business community, higher education, and other professions. There are bookshelves of "how to lead" titles at the local bookstore, lengthy online lists, self-help tools, academic research studies, and "lessons learned" from successful business people just a mouse click away. Many of these characteristics are obvious, while others are less so to artistic leaders; however, many often get overlooked. To lead an arts project, dance company, theater organization, performing arts center, or musical group takes a special balance of personal traits along with a prerequisite of talent.

Through the lens of our collective experiences we have witnessed a number of world-class artist/entrepreneurs who, in one way or another, share some similar leadership characteristics. Some of these traits are imbedded in their DNA and others are learnable. While experience and maturity cannot be replicated for an emerging arts leader, the first steps to enhancing your leadership capacity should be somewhat self-evident and discovered by your personal SWOT analysis you developed earlier. Identifying personal challenges and opportunities is just one step in building your capacity as an arts leader. Over time, you can build off your strengths and build new skills that will provide effective leadership.

The notion that leadership can't be taught or learned is simply not true. Time, experience, and self-discovery will lead you to be an effective leader.

In the arts, we also have an advantage where our talent and creativity will allow us instant credibility that isn't typically available in the corporate world. Leadership in the arts, however, is rarely touched on in an academic setting. Some schools are offering music business and introductory entrepreneurship classes, but there is a need to add leadership and entrepreneurship to the arts core curriculum.

Be assured that there is no magic formula of proven leaderships traits that works the same for everyone. You will need to meld your personal traits with your talent in order to effectively serve as an arts leader. Unfortunately, building a set of leadership qualities for young artists is, at best, accomplished by trial and error.

One popular leadership fallacy that we often hear is you must *lead by example*. This is of course true, but simply leading by example without clearly and enthusiastically communicating your goals does not make a good leader. If you watch great leaders such as Tom Brady, LeBron James, or Duke Ellington, they reached the top of their "game" and are in the conversation for "greatest of all time" by not only consistently demonstrating their own extraordinary talent, but by making everyone around them better. For example, if their shot is not open, LeBron and Steph Curry equally value a great pass that leads to a score as much as a basket. Closely watch Tom Brady run a two-minute drill and you will see inspired leadership—he exudes confidence and a belief that anything is possible. In these sports-related examples, success for the team is the primary goal over any individual accomplishment. As for the artistic leader, the same is equally true.

Transformational arts leaders who inspire new directions in their art or take an existing art form to a new level are legendary. Miles Davis almost single-handedly transformed the direction of jazz, not once or twice, but three times; Bill T. Jones and Martha Graham were trailblazers in dance; and we can look at the work of Picasso, Monet, or Van Gogh to see how their work transformed the future of painting. Likewise, the future of musical theater has been transformed by Lin-Manuel Miranda, Leonard Bernstein, and Stephen Sondheim. And, in big band jazz, listen to how the collective works of Duke Ellington, Count Basie, or the revolution that Benny Goodman began with his epic 1938 recording at Carnegie Hall influenced the future of the art form for all time. Some of these arts leaders utilized a top-down style of dictatorial leadership while others succeeded through a democratic leadership style. In each case, the leader was able to communicate his or her artistic vision, focus on a specific goal, and "drive the bus home."

> **Exercise 8.1**: Write down the most influential artist who has changed your approach to your art and why. What leadership qualities do you admire in this artist?

A THEORETICAL APPROACH TO LEADERSHIP

The arts leadership characteristics we have identified may resonate with some and with others may be a mystery. Regardless, each of our leadership characteristics are important, depending on the *situation*. Much of our thinking has been guided by groundbreaking leadership scholars Paul Hersey and Ken Blanchard, who first described their leadership theory at the Ohio State University in the late 1960s, through several articles and books and titled *Situational Leadership*.

Hersey and Blanchard's premise was simple—you can chart an appropriate style of leadership as indicated by the importance of building relationships or simply completing a task. Hersey and Blanchard build their leadership theory using an *x axis* that measures "relationship" or "supportive behavior," scored from low to high and a *y axis* that measures attention to "task behavior" or "directive behavior," scored from low to high. The *x/y* axes form a chart divided into four matrices, that suggest four basic leadership styles.

Jobs with a low attention to relationships and a low drive to complete a "task" call for a "delegating" style of leadership. When more value is paid to relationship building, but a relatively low drive to completing a task, a "supporting" leadership style is called for. When both relationship building and the completion of a task is crucial, Hersey and Blanchard suggest that a "coaching" style of leadership is appropriate and when there is a strong need to complete a task with little regard to building relationships, the authors state a "directing" style of leadership is called for.

Hersey and Blanchard's work is also informed by a third dimension—the maturity of the group being led. A group of low maturity may inform the style of leadership that is best suited to a particular situation, thus, *Situational Leadership*.

To understand how Hersey and Blanchard's work can be used in practice, you can visualize how a widget-producing factory might need a leader who is responsible for producing as many widgets per hour as possible without any care of building relationships with the widget makers. This would clearly call for a "directing" style of leadership. On the other hand, a long-term project that requires creative artists or performers to perform or complete a project is likely to need a more democratic style of leadership. If, however, the project is due in a certain time frame or the team has a tendency to be immature, a different form of leadership may be required. Thus, the term "situational leadership" is used and can help inform future leaders of basic leadership theory.

In one study a random sampling of band directors and "successful" high school band directors was administered a survey developed by Hersey and Blanchard. The survey suggested that both the successful and randomly selected directors exhibited a "selling" type of leadership within their high school band programs. This indicated a high need for relationship building and a focus on the task at hand. As you can imagine for most educators, there is an overarching care for their students and also a focus on recruitment and retention, all while preparing for the next concert, halftime show, or competition—attention to both task and relationship. The research did indicate that while there were not any significant differences in the directors' leadership behavior, there were statistically significant differences between the directors in regard to demographic data such as band size, budget, school size.

To summarize, Hersey and Blanchard argue that a successful leadership style is dependent on the maturity and needs of those being led and needs to be based on the situation of the group being led. The key point is that artistic leaders should understand that leadership takes many forms and you should approach each leadership opportunity with a conceptual framework that should be nimble—according to your personality and the evolving needs of the group.

The concept of *Servant Leadership* is another valuable way to understand leading your team. Originally coined in the 1970s by Robert K. Greenleaf, it essentially means that a great leader is a servant first. With regard to the arts and your project, the key element for servant leadership is that you are serving the mission and vision of your group and your art. This is why time needs to be devoted to developing clear goals, a personal and artistic inventory, and an artistic vision. Through this process, all of the members of your team are involved and invested in promoting and furthering the shared mission. With a servant leadership style, your strength as a leader comes from more of a moral authority and influence, not from coercion. Everyone is equally serving your artistic vision. This will help guide your artistic and business decision making as your execute your project.

We can also refer you to a number of additional references that can help clarify the qualities of a successful artist/entrepreneur and give a fuller understanding of different approaches to arts leadership needs and styles. Many of these references focus on success in the business world, but as artist entrepreneurs, this is just as relevant for young artists building sustainable careers. The earlier mentioned work by Stephen Covey is excellent source material for understanding general leadership and effectiveness traits. We also recommend *Organizing Genius* by Warren Bennis and Jim Collins' *Good to Great* as excellent source material for young artist/entrepreneurs.

FIVE SPECIFIC TRAITS OF SUCCESSFUL ARTIST/ENTREPRENEURS

There is no doubt the following list could be expanded to ten or even twenty items. The traits we've chosen are most appropriate for Artist Entrepreneurs and encompass many of the "standard" traits you're likely to see in most leadership lists. These traits are ones that we believe will build your capacity as an arts leader and traits that we observe in world-class arts leaders on a daily basis.

1. Artist

At the core of every successful artist entrepreneur is an artist. Whether you are a musician, painter, poet, actor, or dancer—your craft and talent must remain the focus of your life as an entrepreneur. As you navigate the steps needed to build a sustainable career as an artist entrepreneur, a sense of urgency in telling your stories must be coupled with finding new stories to tell. If you only have one story to tell, no doubt you will at some point get bored presenting the work and your artistic tank could run empty. We must constantly explore and think about what we see, the people around us, the landscape, and source material that will inspire our next creative story. For example, many songwriters are able to draw upon personal experiences to help craft new songs; artists travel and immerse themselves in nature and are often inspired by the natural landscape; playwrights often imagine new ways to explore the endless supply of human emotion; choreographers find new avenues to explore our world through the human form; and musicians often explore new sounds, new styles, and new indigenous music to build capacity to tell their next story. In each case, the artists are looking to build their artistic palette, which will help inform their next story and help sustain interest in their next project. Arts leaders must constantly be looking through their individual lens to build their current and future storytelling ability.

2. Unrelenting Work Ethic

Without exception, every successful artist has a laser-focused work ethic that feeds a hunger to succeed and a drive to avoid failure. Virtually every artist we know has gone through the hunger stage—hungry to succeed as an artist, hungry to prove the doubters wrong, hungry to follow your heart into a career that no one said was going to be easy. (See the biographies of Charlie Parker or Eric Clapton for great examples.)

It takes an unrelenting focus on developing your craft and finding your niche to the point where you can monetize your talent. Every professional artist, at some point in their career, finds that stage when obstacles and doubt creep into their dreams of becoming an Artist Entrepreneur.

As we said earlier, we don't subscribe to the notion of the starving artist. If you are (metaphorically) hungry, a successful arts career takes patience and hard work. Nothing is more motivating than fear of failure. When your life as a working artist seems to be in peril is when you need to double down on the work. It will be much easier to give in, find a regular-paying job, and abandon your dreams when you don't have a plan for success. While we obviously don't advocate going into poverty, developing artists need to navigate the times where you might need a job outside the arts, such as a day job, an Uber driver or a Starbucks barista, to make ends meet. Every successful artist goes through this period. From gigging jazz musicians in New York City to singer-songwriters in Nashville to painters trying to sell a painting, we've all heard "no" more often than seems fair to anyone. You have to hear these rejections and the "nos" as "not yet." There is a *determined spirit* to successful artists who are able to fight through the bad times and significant hurdles to building a sustainable arts career. There are dozens of examples that we can point to that give us hope. For example, Walt Disney was fired from his newspaper job for "not being creative enough"; J. K. Rowling and Stephen King received dozens of rejections before their first publication; Beyoncé struggled to get her career started for seven years in the Girl's Tyme band; the first Dr. Seuss manuscript was rejected twenty-eight times; Fred Astaire was told at a casting call that he "can't act, slightly bald, dances a little"; George Lucas wanted to be a race car driver; and Jerry Seinfeld was booed off stage early in his career.

These are just a handful of famous artists who failed at the beginning of their careers. The overarching trait that these and many others exhibited was hard work, a sense of overcoming odds, and an inner drive to succeed.

Exercise 8.2: Research an artist whom you respect and see if you can identify a time when she or he was struggling to make a living as an artist.

3. Communication

The third trait that successful artist entrepreneurs must have is the ability to clearly communicate. As an artist, our goal is to communicate our art to an audience and then, as an Artist Entrepreneur, be compensated for our work. As we present our art to audiences, publishers, casting directors, producers, gallery owners, we need to be able to clearly present our art, discuss the work's meaning, articulate the vision, and "sell" the product. As artists, we need to think of our art as a saleable commodity. We have something someone else can't provide and there is a price to provide the "product." As a trained artist, and one who can give a consumer a product that is needed, there is a market price that you can ask. As you create more demand for your product, there is a price variable that increases. For example, there is much more demand for Drake than for an unknown artist, thus Drake can price his product higher than the unknown. As the demand for a product increases, the price increases—the simple definition of supply and demand.

As you look to succeed as an artist entrepreneur, your ability to communicate with your "consumer," and your ability to negotiate a fair exchange of currency for your product is essential. We go through our formative years focusing on the development of our art without much thought as to how we can forge a sustainable career with our art. As you now dive into the practicalities of building a career, the ability to communicate with the end users is crucial to your success.

FOUR TYPES OF ARTS COMMUNICATION

There are four basic means of communicating that artists should master. First, the ability to *write* clearly and succinctly is somewhat of a lost art in today's world of Twitter and Snapchat. If you struggled with some of the earlier exercises, especially the vision statement presented earlier, you should use every opportunity to improve your writing skills. The secret to good writing is to be succinct, write what you mean, be clear, and do not embellish your words with too many adjectives.

Secondly, the ability to clearly communicate through the *spoken word* is another trait that artists must employ. As you begin to sell your product (art), you will need to negotiate through oral communication and be able to clearly articulate your vision and "asking price." We see so many young artists struggle with oral communication because of a dependence on cell phone communication and a simple lack of practice. In school, you are generally working on your craft and hanging out with your friends with little formal training in oral communication or verbalizing your art. Chances are you haven't had much practice in telling a stranger or potential employer about your craft and why you should be hired. Students in business colleges practice the art of the "elevator pitch" or mock Shark Tank exercises to prepare them for the "real world"—something that emerging artists can work on.

The third style of communication is through *digital* means. It is a skill where millenials and "digital natives" have a relatively high level comfort level. As an artist entrepreneur, the ability to build a website, upload cloud-based material, and/or communicate through digital media are all crucial elements of a successful arts career in the new arts economy.

Finally, the successful artist entrepreneur has to be able to *visually* communicate via various existing and emerging media. Visual communication is different than digital communication in that the visual appearance of your communication has to be clear, focused, and uncluttered. The graphic design of your web pages, social media, and other contemporary communication are crucial and should look professional and be consistent with your artistic vision.

Part of your job as an arts leader is to communicate your vision for the project. As we've articulated earlier, your project is your artistic vision, now you have to execute. Through a strong ability to communicate your vision, motivate your team, and delegate appropriate responsibilities, you now can focus on how best to present your project.

4. Common Sense

To fast-track your path to being an Artist Entrepreneur, you should also understand the simple importance of using common sense. Although it is impossible to emulate the wisdom that comes from years of experience and maturity, emerging artists have the benefit of utilizing mentors, whether in school of practicing professionals. There are active mentoring opportunities that can be tapped into, and through your networks and your school you have the basis to identify and utilize a mentor. In the arts, established artists are almost always willing to help the next generation succeed. All it takes is the time and respectful methods to ask for advice. Many times a former teacher, a clinician who visits your school, or someone you've connected with through social media can serve as the initial point of contact to get connected to a mentor. Seasoned professionals value their ability to share their lessons learned to assist the next generation. You can't get started unless you ask.

> **Exercise 8.3**: Write down names of 2–3 respected professionals and try to contact them with a relevant question about their work that would help the next steps in your career.

Universities do an excellent job in developing talent and artistic skills, however there is no substitute for teaching "common sense," that is the ability to stand back and think about your next steps, your "eyes on the prize" and to keep a focus on how your day-to-day actions will impact your goal of becoming an artist entrepreneur with a sustainable career.

The adage that "it takes a lifetime to build a reputation, and a minute to destroy it" has been proven too many times in today's twenty-four-hour digital news cycle and instant worldwide digital communication. As an Artist Entrepreneur, there is nothing more important than building your reputation—and that includes your work ethic, your honesty, your preparedness and punctuality, and your reliability. We know several artists who live in metropolitan areas and leave nothing to chance if, for example, they face rush hour traffic or public transportation. There is always an contingency plan. Once you miss a gig, even if you couldn't have done anything about it for whatever reason, you likely will move down the list of options for the next opportunity.

People are always observing you even when you're unaware of it.—Marina Lomazov, concert pianist

It's often stated that if you're not fifteen minutes early to a "gig," you're late. This is the gospel truth. I've seen artists burst into a rehearsal or session two to three minutes before a gig, play a few warm-up notes and pretend to be ready to go. The fact is, the pre-rehearsal, pre-performance networking and building of community is often where the next gig comes from. Additionally, I've seen woodwind players still putting together their instruments or getting their reeds in shape as the clock starts. That's a perfect way to not get the next job.—Rick Goodstein

I was told once that conductors learn who they want to play in their ensembles from watching the musicians warm up and prepare for the rehearsal or performance. The point was that conductors want to work with artists who are early and prepared. Remember, at the professional level, everyone is talented. Don't do something to jeopardize your artistic reputation.—Eric Lapin

Common sense also means taking care of yourself. Getting enough exercise, sleep, and the right foods are a tremendous responsibility when sustaining a grueling life in the arts. We all know stories of unbelievable talent that has gone to waste and careers sidetracked by young artists not taking the time to do the right thing—that is, the common sense about taking care of yourself.

At the end of every semester, I take the time to remind my classes and students of this point. You have to sleep and you have to eat. This book is about building a sustainable and long term career in the arts . . . not making you a one-hit wonder. Your health and well-being is essential to building that sustainable career.—Eric Lapin

Growing up in the 1960s and 1970s, my heart still breaks by losing too many great musicians at a young age. Jimi Hendrix, Janis Joplin, and Jim Morrison all come to mind as sad reminders about how young artists who were caught up in the moment and didn't take care of themselves.—Rick Goodstein

Maintaining enthusiasm for your art is another sub-trait of using common sense. Too many times professional artists get jaded by the day-to-day realities of forging a career in the arts. Many promising artists get sidetracked from their potential by developing a surly attitude, bringing baggage to work, or having extraneous or personal problems affect their art. Learning to rise above difficult times when it seems the world is against you is easier said than done. It will, however, allow you to maintain a consistent approach that will be valued by your colleagues.

Common sense also is about being human. Being kind to others and being cheerful and helpful in stressful situations will build on your reputation as an artist and will lead contractors and producers to think about you for the next opportunity. Collegiality is one of our favorite words—being fun to be around, being a good listener, and a caring human being is one of the most precious traits we have complete control over. Don't let a lousy attitude, laziness, or surliness derail your goals—LIFE'S TOO SHORT as it is! There are countless examples of someone with an outstanding attitude toward their work succeeding when a more talented artist with a bad attitude got left behind.

Exercise 8.4: Write down one piece of common sense that you would like to work on over the next month and make a note to look back next month.

5. Motivator

As a leader, you will need to find the balance between being heavy handed and not leading at all. Good leaders are master *motivators*. Sometimes leading from the front is appropriate while a different leadership opportunity requires leadership from the middle. There have been successful leaders who can lead from a dictatorial position while others thrive in a culture of diverse and democratic leadership.

Successful arts leadership cannot be defined into a "one size fits all" box. You will need to understand your own strengths and shortcomings and mold your personality into the situation (situational leadership). The primary goal is to share your vision with your team and to be able to communicate the vision with clarity and purpose. Motivation comes from combining strong communication skills to share your artistic vision, integrity, and common sense. Successful leaders are able to build and maintain a culture that fits their vision of success. As you begin to develop your ideas for your project, build a culture that is molded from your personal "brand." Great examples abound in today's business world, where successful organizations, from small start-ups to corporate behemoths like Google, Coca-Cola, and Apple insist on their culture of innovation, diversity, and shared responsibility to execute the overarching corporate vision.

Small arts organizations, bands, dance companies, and theater troupes can also emulate a shared culture that will develop over time. Building and maintaining a culture is one of the most important elements in building a successful "brand" and one that has defined some of the most creative and successful arts organizations. From Wynton's Jazz at Lincoln Center to Pilobolus to Cirque du Soleil, there is an artistic brand that has been developed and maintained that defines their art the minute you hear the name.

Most successful leaders also intrinsically assist in their motivational skills by maintaining a good dose of humility. Leaders who are "team players" and those who share the successes with their team build accelerated motivation into the ensemble's performance. As a leader, it's your team, and as you build camaraderie, trust, and collective progress toward a common goal, there will be more buy-in from the team. Admitting mistakes, having the ability to laugh at yourself, and a sense of humor goes a long way to helping motivate any group, especially under stressful or challenging circumstances. As the buy-in from your team into your overarching vision grows, you will be more comfortable delegating various responsibilities to the team members. This delegated authority builds additional trust, accelerates progress toward the goal, and shared accountability.

The "underground" tapes of Buddy Rich blowing up at his band on the bus and the tyrannical stories of orchestral conductors Arturo Toscanini and George Szell were tremendous early examples for me of what not to do. The cliche, "you catch more bees with honey than with vinegar," is one of the underlying principles I try to remember as a leader. —Rick Goodstein

---

Young artists can help build their careers by carefully watching and imitating their favorite teachers, mentors, or colleagues. As the adage goes, imitation is the sincerest form of flattery and in our world, emulating role models we witness is one of the best initial steps to building your leadership capabilities.

Like any business, being a professional artist means that you'll need to have a brand and define who and what you plan to present. You will need to figure out the means to make your "brand" enticing without compromising your artistic integrity.

As we have articulated in this chapter, arts leadership takes many forms and through an understanding of leadership theory to modeling the behaviors of your most influential mentors and teachers, you will develop your own personal brand of leadership that fits who you are and your brand.

9

Marketing and the Use of Social Media

Marketing may sound like a very odd topic of discussion when creative projects are involved. Quite the contrary. Imagine that you have created this wonderful masterpiece, but unfortunately, no one is aware of what you've created! This is the dilemma many artists find themselves in. According to Gail Z. Martin in her book, *The Essential Social Media Marketing Handbook*, she asserts the importance of having a *platform* and a *plan*. Ms. Martin suggests that you create your *platform* and your *plan* simultaneously.

We recommend emerging Artist Entrepreneurs take marketing classes and other opportunities to grasp the complexities of social media tools that are available. For most artists, marketing is a topic that is rarely discussed or offered to the arts student. We mentioned earlier how most students (at all levels) in the arts are not usually involved in the business or marketing aspects of performances or events. Students don't usually select the repertoire, reserve the venue, have the posters or programs printed, or engage in any facet of the marketing process. They simply show up and perform, never really knowing how or what was necessary to ensure that the performance venue was full. With the exception of your senior recital or gallery showing, students rarely immerse themselves in the marketing aspects of their college career. Until you are fortunate enough to have your own publicist or marketing team, having a clear understanding of the marketing process is crucial for emerging artist. With universal access to technology and social media platforms, it is much easier to get your message to your public. However, with the proliferation of web marketing and list-serves, there is such easy access to the internet that your message may be buried in the noise. The question becomes how do you distinguish your message from the plethora of other artists who are trying to get their message heard as well? Allow us to offer a few strategies that help answer that question.

Now, the business has changed. When I was coming up in the early 1990s, the only way you could get a job was by someone inviting you in. Now with the Internet and social media you can pretty much make your own film, make your own album, make your own web series. You can do all these things now that were not possible then. So you were really dependent on someone else to call you in. Not anymore. —Michael McElroy, actor

BUILDING YOUR FAN BASE

Building your fan base while establishing your following is one of the most important first steps in developing your marketing strategy. You want people to know who you are and what you're doing. Start with your close circle of friends. Then expand to people in your outer circles. At each performance, have a mechanism for gathering names, email addresses, or other forms of contact information. Many artists simply encourage fans to "like" them on Facebook and follow them on Twitter or Instagram. While this is great, engagement with your social media is the important part. Whenever there is a program for performances, you should list your social media handles in the program. You'd be surprised how quickly you're able to accumulate a broad fan base.

THE WEBSITE

If you have a desire to function as a professional, having a website is a must. Every artist must have a site where prospective presenters and fans can peruse your information and examine your "product" at their leisure. Like we mentioned earlier, the day of mailing out hard copies of your press kits to presenters has long been over. It was very expensive (i.e., printing and mailing costs) and in the new arts economy, a waste and largely ineffective. Not having a website automatically puts you in a league where you will not be considered a serious professional artist. There is no chance that a presenter will book you without a professional social media and website presence. If you don't have the financial resources to hire a website designer, there are a host of basic do-it-yourself programs that will at least allow you to have a presence on the internet.

To build a website for your product, it should contain the following:

Homepage with your photos that describe your act

Menu on the homepage should be easy to navigate with operable "hot" links to:

- Your bio
- Examples of your work (video)
- Photo Gallery
- Contact information
- Blog
- Fan sign-up page
- Merchandise
- Positive reviews and/or testimonials

Think of your website as a living and breathing organism. As your career evolves, so should your website. It should be a clear reflection of you and what you represent as an artist. The key is to craft a website that is welcoming for the viewer and easy to navigate. Since most younger audience members will be engaging with your website on smartphones or tablets, it is essential that your website be mobile friendly. Nothing will turn away a technology native from your art more than a confusing website that isn't compatible with their phone. As you communicate with your fans, be personable; reveal things about you that would be interesting to your fans. Remember that this is your opportunity to engage your audience in a digital conversation. You have to think of your website as a living organism that must be updated and maintained regularly without dated material, information, or dead links. To this end, you have to regularly "feed the monster" that is at the front door of your career. For good examples check out the websites for Clair Bremner, Ranky Tanky, or the Okee Dokee Brothers.

THE BIO

If you are not a very good writer, it will be worth the investment to hire someone who specializes in writing bios for artists. This will be the best $300 you've ever spent in terms of having a professional sing your praises in a very coherent and succinct manner. If you can't afford to hire a professional writer, you should read other well-written bios and mimic their template. Most amateur writers tend to either "pad" their bios with mundane information, such as high school achievements, performing at the local PTA Meeting, Kiwanis Club, or performing at wedding receptions. While those were likely memorable gigs you did at the time and were paid, they are not particularly noteworthy for a professional bio. While in college, list notable performances, or artists you have collaborated with or anything beyond the norm. After you've crafted your bio, have people you trust and respect read your bio. They will hopefully be able to offer valuable feedback to you before you place your information before the public.

Exercise 9.1: Craft your bio and share it with trusted friends and colleagues for feedback.

SOCIAL MEDIA

One of the major challenges with technology and social media, it is forever changing. As of this writing, Facebook has become passé in the eyes of most young people, but still a necessary tool in every artist's marketing tool belt. That is, people between the ages of thirteen and thirty have moved to other platforms. However, it still has appeal to an older demographic, those thirty-five and older. There is still tremendous benefit using Facebook, especially having the ability to target your audience. While you want to maintain a personable persona on your social media platform, no one really cares what you had for lunch, how much you love your puppy or Christmas in New York City. Your social pages should contain content that reflects your artistry. It should either contain information about your next performance or photos of the performance you just finished. Maybe you can get a testimonial from a fan or post short clips of your sound check. Maybe you are able to give your fans a behind the scenes experience with Facebook "live." Anything that would be of interest to your fans or presenters would be worthy of a post. The key is to present yourself as the professional you purport to be.

SOUNDCLOUD/YOUTUBE CHANNEL

You may be familiar with the music of Chance the Rapper. He was able to launch an entire career without the service of a record label. He simply uploaded his music and made it available to his fans and the rest, as they say, is history. For the musician, this is one of the most effective ways of getting your music to the public. For your fans and presenters, they want to hear your music and see your stage persona. Having a SoundCloud and a YouTube channel is a must. You're likely not to have a film production team, so footage from your iPhone will suffice until you're able to invest in a more elaborate platform. Nowadays, if you have a laptop computer and a decent microphone, you're able to produce relatively high-quality recordings. These recordings and videos are not necessarily meant to be products that you would sell; rather, they are intended to give your fans and presenters a snapshot of your artistry.

PHOTO SHARING AND BLOGGING

Nothing tells your story with more clarity than adding photos of your artistry. When you combine photos with commentary, your "story" becomes even more compelling. Snapchat, Instagram, and Pinterest tend to cater more toward a younger demographic, so it is important to figure out which platform is best suited for your art. Additionally, there is a significant potential audience on Twitter that can be reached.

LINKEDIN

While LinkedIn seems to be designed primarily for business connections, artists can still use it effectively, especially those who have an educational slant to their artistry. If you pay for the full service, this platform allows you to find like-artists, thus allowing you to build on your connections. This platform is especially useful for building relationships among professionals.

One thing for sure is that technology is always rapidly changing. By the time of this publication, there will already be new innovative ways of connecting with your fans and presenters. The key for artists is to maintain knowledge of the quickly evolving platforms that will effectively promote their artistry. The demographics of your fan base should influence which platform you use. As mentioned earlier, some platforms cater to the post-millennial generation versus an older population. This is where it is important to know your niche market. There are a host of books written that will go into much more detail on how to hone your social media skills. In today's market, artists will need to have a wide array of skills beyond their artistic prowess. Other platforms to consider: Ozone, Weibo, Reddit, Pinterest, Ask.fm, Tumblr, Flickr, VK, Odnoklassniki, and Meetup. As technology continues to evolve, the one constant that can be counted on is change. Artists have to pay attention to the exponential rate of change.

ADVANCE MARKETING

In past years, it was customary for the artists to simply show up for a performance or artistic engagement. Sadly, those days are over. When you have been booked for any performance or showing, it becomes a partnership between you and the hosting venue. This is especially true when showcasing in smaller venues. While we presume that all presenters are lovers of art, their job often depends on the bottom line or business aspects of their programming. It doesn't matter how wonderful and creative your presentation is if it does not attract an audience. Often times, presenters will only measure success by the number of "butts" in the seats. For emerging artists this is most important that you be proactive in mounting a marketing campaign for your concerts and events. Here are several tasks artists can and should do to advance the performance date.

- Arrange radio or newspaper interviews prior to the show
- Ask for the show to be reviewed by local newspaper or bloggers
- Target marketing via Facebook, Instagram, and Twitter
- Invite other presenters from the area to your event

NEWSLETTERS AND MASS MAILING

Newsletters and e-media can be an effective way of staying in contact with your fans and prospective presenters. The key is to have a substantial database of both fans and presenters, which you should now have in your Excel database. The key is to have compelling content. Everyone's time is valuable, so you want to give your reader a reason for wanting to read your newsletter. Content should include upcoming major performances of note, tour schedule, or a new collaboration with another artist. This is the kind of content that gives your newsletter value. Think of your newsletter as a time for you to share your accomplishments with a friend. You're not bragging about what you've done or plan to do, you're simply sharing in a very calm "oh by the way" moment. Thinking of every performance as an opportunity to build your career and an audience for your art, rather than just another gig, is a state of mind that will help you get through the day-to-day grind of being a professional.

Two of the best platforms to address mass mailings are to *MailChimp* or *Constant Contact*. There are others, but these two seem to be the most popular. As previously mentioned, one of the most important features for both platforms is that they allow you, if constructed correctly and constantly maintained, to personalize how you address your fans. That is, your greetings would say, "Dear Samantha" rather than, "Dear Friend." Right away, you have enhanced your chances of having your newsletter read by a prospective fan or presenter. Both platforms allow you to monitor who and when your email was read and how many links were opened. It is always a good idea to have multiple "hot" links embedded in your newsletter. These links should include active links to your website, YouTube channel, or any other pertinent information that will entice your reader to remain engaged.

The next key is to determine how often should you engage in mass e-mailings. Again, there is a thin line between persistence and being annoying. There is no magic answer to that question. The amount of activity you have as an artist will often dictate the frequency of your newsletter. When things are slow and nothing significant has taken place in your artistic life since the last newsletter, then there is no reason to produce another newsletter. When you reach a point where your activity is so ubiquitous, that is usually a sign that you are finally ready for a manager and publicist.

10

We Got the Gig!
Now What?

You have either worked with your agent or you have booked a series of performances or showings yourself. Your website is informative and all of your collateral materials offer a true picture of your creative project. We assume that you have maintained your high level of artistry. Your music, theatrical work, dance, or exhibit is in peak performance shape. You are anticipating a very successful ten-week tour or showing, yet your work in making sure everything goes smoothly is just beginning. In the twenty-first century just being booked for the performance is not enough. Unless you have a team handling your business, you'll need to be just as vigilant about the business aspects as you are about the artistic.

In this chapter, we want to address the part that may not be as exciting as being on stage performing, but are absolutely essential to ensure that everything goes well with the performance, travel, showing, and the tour.

I was going to feed myself by creating my own opportunities. —Michael McElroy, actor

---

BOOKING THE REGIONAL TOUR

Touring is a necessary aspect for every artist. You've got to take your art to the people. Sometimes that will mean performing in large concert halls in major cities or presenting in a gallery for a small town that deserves to have art in their community as well.

What you're paying for is the inconvenience of traveling to your venue. That might include everything from stale peanuts on airlines to hotel rooms not ready upon arrival to flight cancellations. All of these unforeseen issues can make for inconvenient moments while on tour, but that is part of the tour process.

Most tours start with what is known as an "anchor" date. We'd like to expound more on the idea of block booking that was addressed in Chapter 6. These dates are typically the first and most substantial date that will allow the artist to build additional concert dates around the anchor date. It is advised to contact other concert venues notifying them that you're going to be in the area. Offering what is known as "en-route fees," will make your presentation financially more attractive to most presenters. As you engage in block booking for a tour, you may not be able to receive the same fees as your anchor date. Sometimes while on tour, you may encounter an open date. When those days occur, you can book additional dates that will be at a lesser fee, which will make your presentation more acceptable to some venues that may not have the same budget as your original venue. In addition, most venues will have a clause in the contract prohibiting artists from booking another concert date within at least a fifty-mile radius of their venue. For example, if you book a concert in Kansas City, you could ostensibly book concerts in St. Louis, Wichita, and/or Des Moines. The goal should be to fly into large cities where the flight expenses are not as exorbitant as some of the smaller regional airports. This would allow you to fly into Kansas City, rent a car or tour bus, and drive to the other locations. The advantages of this kind of "block booking" allow you to maximize your profits. Block booking allows the artist to schedule a series of performances within a region thus allowing maximized opportunities.

THE CONTRACT

You or your representative has verbally agreed with the presenter on a performance date, location, time, and performance fee. Now, it is time to formalize your agreement with a written and signed contract by both parties. It is best to have the presenter sign the contract first so that all of the items agreed by both parties cannot be altered.

Gone are the days of having a gentlemen's agreement that only involves a handshake to cement a deal. To use the words of former president Reagan, "trust, but verify." Not having a written and signed contract could potentially open both the presenter and the artist up to all kinds of liability issues. In short, the contract should outline every pertinent detail of the agreement made by the presenter and the artist. The contract is usually accompanied with the technical rider. We'll discuss this in more detail later. If you do not have management, it would be worth the investment to hire an entertainment attorney to craft a template of a contract that should be used each time a performance has been booked. Having a written contract will alleviate any ambiguity regarding the terms of your agreement with the presenter.

THE TECHNICAL RIDER

This is another document that every presenter should approve before the contract has been signed. Having a detailed tech rider will help alleviate any misunderstandings with the presenter regarding all aspects of your performance from housing, transportation, food, lighting, sound. Some artists take the tech rider extremely seriously, right down to the brand of bottled water, color of flowers in the green room, or by requesting only green M&M's. Some artists even refuse to perform if any portion of the technical rider is not addressed. We don't recommend that level of "diva" status. Ninety-nine percent of presenters will do everything possible to make the artist as comfortable as possible. It is always important to find a solution rather than go ballistic if one part of the tech rider is not met. Remember that you are building and developing relationships for future gigs and projects as you are working with the venue presenter and production staff. If you are also functioning as your own road manager, we recommend having a conversation with the tech director prior to the event.

The most important thing is to have as much specificity in the technical rider as possible. It is much easier to scale back on equipment (depending on the size of the venue) rather than asking for equipment after the fact. If you are requesting additional equipment or accommodations once you arrive at the venue, the answer more than likely will be, "No, I'm sorry we can't accommodate that request." See appendix for examples of music, theater, and dance technical riders.

ADVANCING THE DATE

We must be constantly reminded that art is also a business. Art presenters' role is to curate and present high-quality artistic presentations while remaining fiscally solvent. While most venues will have their own marketing department, sometimes they may not have time or the expertise to offer the kind of TLC your show demands. Therefore, the artist should be equally (if not more so) invested in the success of the show's attendance. At least four to six weeks before you arrive, it is good to do what is called advancing the date. No matter whether you are presenting your show at a jazz club, your dance at a large college auditorium, your play at a community theater, or your sculpture at a local art gallery, your goal is to have a packed house. Gone are the days when you're booked for a performance or showing and you simply showed up and performed. Today's artists have an obligation to be engaged in the artistic and financial success of the presenter. The artistic part is a given, but the financial part is helping make sure that there are warm bodies in the seats.

ARRANGE FOR INTERVIEWS

It is important to do everything possible to "drum up" as much interest in your show as possible, prior to the performance. There are a host of things that can and should be done prior to your arrival.

Here are two strategies to consider:

NEWSPAPER INTERVIEWS

Contact the local newspaper(s) to arrange for an interview giving you the opportunity to discuss your artistic creation and what the audience can expect to see and hear. Keep in mind that you should be well versed in discussing the aspects of your creation that will resonate with an audience. This is your time to sell your product. In many ways, this pitch will be similar to the same pitch you may have used to convince a donor to invest in your art or convince a presenter to host your show. Direct the interviewer to your website prior to the interview.

Hopefully, they will have done their homework and ask questions that help to further inform and encourage an audience to attend your show. Think of the interview as simply having a conversation with a dear friend discussing your art. It should be comfortable and natural. If you've never done this before, we recommend having a mock interview session with a friend. Craft a series of questions you think might be asked and see if you can speak convincingly and intelligently about your art. We'd also recommend recording this mock session. You'll be surprised how many times you might find yourself beginning each sentence with the word, "like" or "um." You probably want to avoid any kind of "slang" speech that might not translate well during the course of the interview. In addition, you want to avoid any kind of insider language that will only serve to alienate potential patrons. This is a good time to really hone your speaking skills if you're not accustomed to speaking in public or being interviewed. You may ask, "What does this have to do with my art? My art can speak for itself!" That may be true, but what we've learned is, the person who is able to clearly articulate the dimensions of their creative project is the person who comes across as a polished professional.

Exercise 10.1: Plan and execute your mock interview.

It is always a good idea to provide the interviewer with as many video excerpts or recorded examples of your creation as possible. This will better inform the interviewer and help them to ask more informed questions.

Having your performance reviewed by the local arts writer will provide more content (assuming the review is positive) for your website. You should always be thinking about the next performance. When calling the newspaper, ask if the artistic writer would be available to review the concert.

THE RADIO INTERVIEW

Many of the same techniques you used for the newspaper interview can and should be applied to the radio interview. This interview should be arranged at least two to three weeks prior to the performance date. Although, the actual interview may not occur until the day before the event. If your performance is music, hopefully, you've forwarded sample recordings of your project so that excerpts can be played during the course of the interview. In most instances, the interview will be "live" and conducted over the telephone. If that is the case, try to use a landline to avoid the possibility of the call being dropped with a mobile phone. If all you have is a mobile phone, make sure you are in a location where the signal is strong. Speak clearly and slowly so that your listening audience will be able to understand your every word.

COLLEGES AND UNIVERSITIES

Sometimes presenting at colleges and universities can be somewhat tricky. It can be difficult to compete with the vast number of activities that take place on college campuses.

It is best to look at college campuses as a community of people with a variety of backgrounds and varied artistic tastes. To that end, when advancing the date, it is good to target certain departments and faculty within the university that are likely to embrace your particular artistic endeavor. It is also helpful to encourage professors to offer incentives for students to attend your event. Often, faculty will have students craft a summary of the event for extra credit. In some cases colleges will have a number of required events that students must attend. Find out if your concert can be added to the list of required concerts. These kinds of incentives help you to build your following on college campuses. We can point to many artists who were able to capitalize on developing a relationship with college students that lasted for generations. The jazz artist Dave Brubeck is someone who started performing at college campuses in the 1950s. The student relationships that he was able to cultivate during that period remained fans for the rest of their lives. Comedian and talk show host Ellen DeGeneres also got her start performing on college campuses. Colleges are fertile grounds for cultivating life-long fans.

Finally, most college campuses also have a campus newspaper and sometimes an active radio station. Contact both of those offices in an effort to get some advanced publicity.

HOW ABOUT THE COMMUNITY?

Most college campuses also have relationships with the community. When we mention community, that includes the local high schools, other area colleges, social organizations, churches, and even businesses are all fertile areas for helping to build an audience. Because student activity fees support many events on a college campus, the events are often free and open to the public.

Other considerations:

LOGISTICS

Besides the artistic presentation, the organization and planning of your event is crucial to the success of your artistic enterprise. The logistics of moving people from Point A to Point B if not planned well can create a disaster and could have a negative impact on your performance. Not having the proper equipment or accommodations also can have a negative impact on the overall success of your performance.

THE ITINERARY

If you are traveling with an ensemble of dancers, thespians, artists, or musicians, it is important that there be a written document that will provide all of the pertinent information available to each member of the ensemble.

The itinerary should have the following information:

- Name and address of the venue
- Name and phone number(s) of the event host
- Names and phone numbers of each ensemble member
- Flight and travel information of each ensemble member
- Name, address, and phone numbers of hotel with confirmation numbers
- Detailed events with time and location(s)—including sound check, meals, load-in, concert time, etc.

MERCHANDISE

A business model for many artists, particularly those in the music field, is to in many instances post their music online (for free) with the intent of building a fan base that will lead to "live" shows. In the midst of presenting their "live" shows the artists are able to capitalize on the sale of their merchandise. The merchandise may include CDs, digital downloads, T-shirts, caps, mugs, buttons, and so on. Usually, most venues will have a 20 percent venue fee if you sell your merchandise and 30 percent commission if the venue's staff is in charge of selling your merchandise. If you are having someone from your team selling merchandise, it is best to have platforms that will accept credit cards (i.e., Square, Flint, etc.). Make sure your signage is clear with prices of your merchandise and the fact that you accept all major credit cards. You should also try to set up your stand in a location where there is the busiest audience traffic flow. For emerging artists, it is customary to mention from the stage that you do have items for sale for a nominal fee. This too can help direct your fans to your merchandise table.

IT'S TAX TIME!

Dealing with taxes can sometimes become very cumbersome, but if not done properly can cause a host of problems you cannot begin to imagine. "Uncle Sam" will get his money one way or the other! For that reason alone, you want to be on top of all of the tax laws that pertain to your business and how you should address issues with your ensemble members.

WHY FORM AN LLC?

Without getting too deep in the weeds about the pros and cons of the LLC, we would like to offer a few good reasons why artists should consider forming an LLC (Limited Liability Corporation). Two reasons for forming an LLC is that it does offer fewer corporate formalities and there is greater tax flexibility.

However, perhaps the greatest reason is that the LLC provides limited liability protection should a lawsuit arise. In other words, your personal assets will be protected. We suggest you meet with your tax consultant to determine which is the best route for you to explore.

W-9 TAX FORMS

This is particularly important when you are paying the members of your ensemble. Members who receive $600 or more within a tax year MUST complete a W-9 tax form, thus allowing you to forward a 1099 tax form. By law, all of your ensemble members should receive a 1099 form at the beginning of the year (January).

ACCURATE RECORDS

Maintaining accurate books is essential to ensure there are fewer problems come tax time. This is not an advertisement for QuickBooks or any other software program, but this type of software will save you both time and money, and your tax preparer will love you for being able to present them with accurate showings of your complete income and expenses for a given tax year. If you prefer to use an Excel spreadsheet, both platforms should have detailed information about your income and expenses. The names and amounts of stipends paid, travel, hotel, meals expenses, rental car, and so on, should be listed in addition to the income from performance fees, royalties, merchandise sales. Both platforms will execute all of the calculations. You only need to input the data. Having this kind of detailed information will make life easier for you and your tax preparer.

WHILE AT THE SHOW, MANNERS MATTER

As we stated earlier, in the arts business, we have a supply and demand issue. There are more supplies than there is demand. There are simply too many great artists for presenters to put up with poor behavior. This is especially true for emerging artists. When you arrive at a venue for a performance, think of yourself as being a guest in someone else's home. You would think that this topic should not be necessary, but you might be surprised how some artists have sabotaged their chances of repeated performances or being hired by another venue once the word is out to stay clear of them. Yelling at the sound engineer, trashing a hotel room, or being rude to the host presenter does nothing to enhance your performance. It only creates a toxic "vibe" where nobody wins. The artistic world is too small and good and bad news travels very fast. We're all familiar with stories where major artists were fired for "diva-like" behavior. Kathleen Battle being dismissed from the Metropolitan Opera back in 1994 was one of the more high-profile dismissals. Ms. Battle was allegedly dismissed for "unprofessional actions." There are a host of lesser-known acts who (for whatever reason) are not invited back for an encore performance. In most cases, the artist who behaved poorly will not be notified of their behavior. They simply will not be invited back for additional performances. Usually, presenters will talk to each other about the poor behavior of a particular group. That kind of bad press can and will impact future performances. If you are the leader of your ensemble, it is imperative that you remind members that their actions are a reflection of your brand. If there is a problem with any aspect of the logistics while on tour, you as the leader should be the person to resolve those kinds of matters.

Illegal drugs and/or excessive alcohol use are a huge no-no! Again, this should be obvious, but some artists will find themselves in a situation where things can quickly get out of control. This kind of indulgence can quickly derail a career. The goal for every artist is to be welcomed back for an encore performance and to establish a reputation for their artistic prowess and being good citizens.

11

Funding Your Project

So you went through the creative process. You did your table talk sessions, you identified your artistic DNA, you practiced quiet time, and of course you have spent years diligently honing your craft and have a "big idea" project you believe will launch your career. Now you need some support. We've talked about hiring professional writers for your bio, hiring a designer for your website, and maybe bringing on a social media coordinator. On top of that, we've mentioned that showcase performances can cost up to $3,000. Even if you personally handle aspects of your career such as the accounting, the bio, website, or the social media yourself, doing these things in a professional manner still costs money. So the next step in this process is, can I get funding for my project?

GRANT FUNDING

Grants are an excellent way to financially support your project. Grants come in all sizes, can fund many different aspects of your work, and can be found from a variety of sources such as federal and state agencies, public and private foundations, and local governments. Grants are not loans, and can provide you with an opportunity to fund specific elements of your work while freeing up your time and finances to focus on other necessary business or creative matters.

The first step in identifying and applying for grant funding was actually covered much earlier. You first have to know who you are, what your goals are, and what your project is. Having clear goals and an artistic vision will help ground your funding search. All granting organizations have a mission, and by knowing your own mission and goals, you'll be able to find grant funding from organizations where your missions align. National organizations such as the National Endowment for the Arts and the National Endowment for the Humanities tend to be interested in broad impact—how many people are you able to impact through your project? State and local arts organizations (California Arts Council, SC Arts Commission) are going to be more likely to support new artists developing and working on a regional, state, or municipal level. Regional arts organizations (South Arts, Arts Midwest, Western States Arts Federation) are going to be looking for projects that impact their specific region. Charitable Foundations (Doris Duke, Bill and Melinda Gates, Carnegie) often have very specific goals in mind. This might be something like STEM education, promoting new art, or diversifying audiences. Lastly, corporations are often an option. They are more likely to focus on projects that offer their business positive marketing and PR. With any of these, you do not want to try to stretch or focus your artistic mission to fit the call for grant proposals. In doing so, you may sacrifice your creative integrity (also covered earlier) and compromise your project, but not necessarily. Grant award decisions are made by professionals in the field who will easily see through an attempt to significantly alter your project to fit the grant. This will be seen as manipulative. In short, stay true to your artistic DNA and creative vision.

Once you know who you are, you have to know who they are. Who will be reading your proposal. Is this being read by highly educated professionals in your specific field? Or is it being read by a cultural arts council where the reviewers may not know as much about your specific arts discipline or project? This process of identifying your audience will help you choose language that best presents your project. In the arts we have a broad range of discipline-specific language that may not be appropriate for all grant reviewing audiences. A confused reviewer is unlikely to recommend your proposal for funding. Ensure that your proposal is clear, succinct, and accurately represents your art.

Grant writing is a process. We've talked already about how writing is a necessary communication skill for an Artist Entrepreneur. Under no circumstances should you submit the first draft of your proposal. That's just not how writing works. It's a process where you outline your proposal, create a first draft, have trusted friends and colleagues review, and revise, revise, revise.

Proofreading and editing for clarity take place throughout all stages of the process. You also should not waste time applying for a grant that you are not qualified for. Granting agencies typically have very specific qualifications for applications and you will need to find and adhere to these. For example, a grant might (in small print) state that applications will only be accepted by residents of a certain city, county, or state.

While engaged in the writing process, it's worthwhile to remember that the goal of a grant proposal is to present your idea as clearly and concisely as possible. In most cases, you are tasked with explaining your project within a specified format, always with a word count, page limit, or character limit. So, it is important for you to have others read your work who are unfamiliar with your project. Because they don't know about your project, they will be able to give valuable feedback on the clarity of your writing.

Your grant proposal is not a text, email, or social media post. It is important to present yourself and your project professionally. (Yes, this means avoiding emojis.) You will also want to avoid slang and pop culture expressions. In other words, don't say that your project is "lit." Also, while most grants will specify style or have text boxes for input, if you are typing your proposal, make sure to use easy to read and clear font, size, and formatting. Unless otherwise specified (which it often is), we recommend 12 point, Times New Roman. Standard use of punctuation and capitalization should also be adhered to. nO ReVieWeRS WanT tO REaD A pRoPosAL lIke ThiS. This clarity and professionalism also extends to the type of language you are using. Avoid using hyperbole and superlatives. Promoting your project as "the best performance that has ever been created in the history of the world" or "a visual art experience that would make Michelangelo's David look like child's play" is going to be more likely to get your proposal deleted than funded. Use concise language to clearly and professionally explain your idea and why you deserve the funding. Yes, you want to be excited and enthusiastic about your project, but don't sacrifice clarity. Lastly, use an active voice throughout the proposal. An active voice (instead of passive) will typically make your narrative stronger, clearer, and more concise. Consider the differences:

Passive: The clarinet was played by Eric.

Active: Eric played the clarinet.

Budgeting is another essential component. No granting agency will award money without a detailed budget. Remember that granting agencies want to ensure that their funding is being used effectively and efficiently in support of their mission. If the granting organization has a focus to present new theatrical works, they want to see that you are using your award effectively toward that goal. Everything must be accounted for and specifically detailed. Do not be vague. For example, you may need to detail specific amounts for marketing and publicity, mounting the performance, renting a space, and so on. Items such as a massive post-performance party are not acceptable and likely will diminish chances for approval.

Your application should ask for specific dollar amounts within the scope of the grant instead of "about $500." That will be interpreted as a lack of attention to detail. In addition, many grants expect you or your organization to have some financial buy-in. So instead of just handing you money, most granting agencies will expect you to match their contribution in some way. These are presented as ratios for how much each of you are contributing. A 1:1 match means that you put up $1,000 and they put up $1,000. A 2:1 match means that you put up $2,000 and they put up $1,000. Having a financial stake in the project helps to ensure your accountability. Your side of the match can be met through a variety of performance-related expenses: travel, production costs, equipment maintenance, supplies, showcase fees, employee salaries, marketing materials. Your match requirement will vary from agency to agency, and often is just cold hard cash.

We talked earlier about Artist Entrepreneurs being performers, composers, pedagogues, and intellectuals. Well, part of being an intellectual implies understanding the artistic, social, and political climate of the times. Many granting organizations (e.g., NEA, NEH) have their budgets set by Congress. This money then filters down to state arts organizations (e.g., state arts commissions or councils). Artists can easily find the annual funding levels of the state arts commissions and federal granting agencies such as the NEA or NEH. This will help you develop a budget for your proposal that is both responsible and realistic. If funding was down dramatically for the NEA, that means that available grant funds will be down dramatically. So you can develop a proposal that takes into account these changes. When making your budget and total amount requested, remember that arts professionals in a variety of disciplines will be reviewing your proposal. Do not try to pad your budget and ask for more money than you need. Again, the reviews will see your artistic integrity compromised and will move on to the next proposal.

Deadlines are deadlines. Submitting grants is very much a reflection of your professionalism and attention to detail. There is no leeway to beg or plead for an extension. Especially at bigger organizations or foundations, funding agencies will be reviewing thousands of proposals. So be prepared. One of your earliest steps in the grant writing process should be to incorporate all deadlines into your calendar, to-do lists, and short-term goals. These calendars, lists, and goals (each developed in earlier exercises) will help you stay on top of deadlines. If a proposal is due by 5:00 p.m. on January 31, a submission on February 1 will not be accepted, period.

The next step is to be patient. Remember that the larger granting agencies are reviewing proposals that will total in the millions. It is not uncommon to have to wait months for a response from a national organization. For example, an NEA grant submitted in February will typically not have a response until November.

If you do not get the grant proposal funded. Don't panic. No one receives 100 percent of the grants for which they apply. In fact, for federal and corporate granting agencies, the percentages are very low. Remember we've said many times that "no means not right now." If you receive feedback (and you often do), study it closely and incorporate it into the self-reflection process discussed earlier. It's okay not to get the grant. That happens. Just make sure that you learn from the process and feedback.

SUCCESS!

If you do receive funding, the next step will be to execute the grant contract. The contract will specify exactly how the grant money is to be used, how it will be paid, how the granting agency is to be recognized (an important detail), and the time frame in which the funds need to be spent. This contract will again be due back to the agency by a certain date. Failure to return the contract will mean you forfeit your grant award. So, immediately add the contract to your to-do list and calendar.

While executing the terms of the contract, keep detailed financial records and an activity log. Most granting organizations will want records (and sometimes specific examples) of how you recognized them. Some will mandate their logo be on programs, or mentioned in advertising, or referenced on social media. Oftentimes, you will be required to notify governmental representatives (like your state senator and/or state house representative) of your award. These financial records and an activity log/timeline will be essential in completing your Final Report, or Impact Report. All granting agencies will require a final report to be submitted at the end of the granting period. This report will detail how you spent the funds, how you recognized the granting agency, and who you reached with their funding. The due date for this report will be specified in your grant contract. Failure to submit your final report will most often result in you being ineligible for future grants from that organization. Granting organizations have long memories and an artist cannot afford to not pay attention to details and execute the mandates of the grant.

Remember how there is a supply and demand problem for artists? Well that challenge extends to competing for grants. It means that there are a lot of qualified artists all seeking the same funding. If you can't meet your deadlines and requirements professionally, there are plenty more artists who are lined up to receive that funding instead of you.

Exercise 11.1: Go research local, state, and national grants to see where your project may have some funding opportunities. Make a list of possibilities and place due dates on your calendar.

CROWDSOURCING
We've mentioned before that an artist entrepreneur must be current and fluent with emerging technologies. The ability to harness the power of the internet is essential in your marketing and publicity efforts. It can also be an exceptionally powerful tool in your quest for funding. Crowdsourcing is the process of using the internet to solicit funds from your followers (friends, family, or fans) to fund your project. With the proliferation of social media and websites, this strategy has become incredibly popular among emerging artists. As a result, there are no shortages of available platforms to help manage this process. Platforms like Kickstarter and GoFundMe are two popular sites among countless others that will help manage this funding option. While this can be a very effective means of financially powering your project, there are some pros, cons, and risks.

First, the pros. Through the power of social media and the internet, you can bring your project idea to thousands of potential supporters. This reach can mean you almost effortlessly expand your database (which you have developed earlier). Because of this enormous reach, for you to reach your funding goal, you do not need to ask people for large dollar amounts. In fact, typically, the funding power of crowdsourcing comes from small donations from individual donors. These $5, $10, and $20 donations are as much in support of you as they are for your project. But because you are reaching so many people through social media, small donations will add up. The ability to donate a small amount means that money is rarely prohibitive. Whereas a friend or family member may not be able to easily give you $500 for new art supplies, they can probably afford to give you $5.

Crowdsourcing is easy. Online platforms and payment methods allow your supporters to easily send you money. Especially among digital natives this process is incredibly simple. In others words, you can easily solicit small donations from a very wide range of supporters. Finally, crowdsourcing enables you to solicit donations for very specific needs. Instead of simply raising funds to support your dreams, you are raising a specific dollar amount needed, for example, to fund your showcase at APAP. Your supporters now feel more like part of the team. Donors enjoy being able to know what they specifically supported.

There are, however, some cons. One challenge with crowdsourcing is that it has become ubiquitous online. People launch campaigns to cover medical bills, pay for a wedding, pay for college, and yes, support their artistic endeavors. Many national charitable organizations, such as the Red Cross and the United Way, have sophisticated fundraising operations, so your crowdfunding project will have competition. The fact is that your friends, family, and fans are being solicited often for a variety of well-meaning causes. The advantage of crowdsourcing is that you are only asking for small donations. Regardless it is still asking a lot of your fans. Along those lines, you can only crowdsource your funding needs so often. You cannot continue to go back to the same well asking for money. You will give those following you on your social media platforms and website "donor fatigue." As should seem obvious, crowdsourcing is not a viable long-term funding strategy for your project. Ultimately, the goal is to use the crowdsourced funds to turn your art into a financially sustainable presentation.

As is obvious, you cannot effectively crowdsource without a professional website and social media channels. Crowdsourcing is powered through the reach that the internet provides. If your online presence isn't already effective in promoting your message, then your crowdsourcing attempt will be unsuccessful. Also, like granting agencies, your friends, family, and fans want to know what they are giving money to. The most effective crowdsourcing examples are centered around stories. If you have a clear artistic vision and goals, you are more likely to inspire others to support you. Lastly, be specific. Crowdsource funding must be focused on a specific event, item, or project. It is not a general donation to fund your life.

TRADITIONAL FUNDRAISING

As an individual Artist Entrepreneur, traditional fundraising campaigns may not be your best option. Previously, many donors who would typically give to charitable causes would be expecting a tax write-off for their gift. Today, the 2017 tax reform has disallowed many smaller tax write-offs under the 501(c)(c) Internal Revenue Service. In the new arts economy, "traditional" fundraising may not be the best way to obtain funding for your project.

Regardless, traditional fundraising campaigns typically involve identifying a set of donors, targeting them through a variety of media, offering gifts or donor perks, and saying thank you. However, as your enterprise grows, these more traditional fundraising methods will undoubtedly become more sustainable than crowdsourcing. For this reason, keeping your contacts up to date continues to be an essential component of your artistic and business development.

Your first job will be to target a more specific set of potential donors. Unlike crowdsourcing, where you throw your plea out on the internet, in a traditional campaign, you send out emails, make phone calls, or send out direct mail pieces to specific targets or potential donors. This list of potential donors should stem from contact information collected at your performances or events. This is why it is essential to have a means for collecting as much contact information from your fans and patrons at events. Since you can't email, call, or mail everyone, this database of fans and supporters will be more likely to continue to support your work.

Next, develop a message. Just like in a crowdsourcing campaign, you will need to articulate a clear narrative about what your donors are supporting. Again, no one wants to just give you money. Patrons want to know what they are supporting. Here, clarity and transparency will be essential. If your campaign seems vague or confusing, your fans are not going to give their money to your project. Just like in a crowdsourcing campaign, the more of a personal connection to your work your patrons feel, the more likely they are to help.

A good fundraising campaign is going to target donors through multiple forms of media. Unlike a crowdsourcing solicitation, in traditional fundraising, you will utilize social media, emails, phone calls, direct mail, and donor events to sell your narrative and make your pitch. The important word here is "and." By utilizing all of the different methods together, you maximize your opportunity to connect your message with your patrons. This plan must be organized on a fundraising calendar. Just like at a restaurant where you do not want your salad and entree to arrive together, you should plan your different fundraising materials so that they don't all arrive at the same time. By spacing them out, you have the opportunity to consistently deliver your message pitch to your donors through a variety of media.

You must also consider any perks you are going to offer you donors. Typically, you will offer enhanced perks as the donor gift goes up. This is where it is important to know your donors. These perks may include behind the scenes experiences, physical gifts (T-shirts, pins, flash drives, hats, etc.), or opportunities for early ticket purchases. Really, it just needs to be whatever would incentivize your patrons to give.

Lastly, the thank you is essential. Another term for fundraising is development. A heartfelt and genuine thank you will help you *develop* stronger relationships with your fans and donors. The thank you does not need to be elaborate or extravagant, but it does need to happen. Your thank you can include phone calls, follow up emails, recognition on social media or your website, or special recognition at your next event. And everyone still loves a written thank-you note. Through these different formats, you should express your appreciation for their support, give a quick overview of what their gift helped fund, and a quick snapshot of your latest work. All of these different types of thank yous should be as personal as possible. Under no circumstances should you forget this last step. Without an appropriate thank you, you are all but guaranteeing a one-time gift, and a lost fan.

MONEY MANAGEMENT

A crucial step in managing the money you have brought in to help support your art is to maintain accurate records. This includes detailing all of your expenses and generated revenue. Keeping accurate receipts and expense records will serve two purposes. Most immediately, it will enable you to submit accurate accounts of your expenses for grant final reports and be valuable when it is time to prepare your tax returns. In the long term, maintaining your project expenses will allow you to track the true costs of your artistry. In doing so, you will be able to make better financial decisions for your artistic future. These expenses should be broken down in as much detail as possible. The more detail, the more data you have to make these financial decisions. Breaking down travel costs (rental car, hotel, meals, etc.) for an out-of-town gig will ultimately provide you with better information than just a generic total cost figure. We mentioned earlier that understanding and being able to navigate Excel spreadsheets is an essential Artist Entrepreneur skill in today's arts economy. You can attempt to track and manage these necessary expense reports yourself.

However, there is also a lot of help available. Programs, organizations, and software are available to help you manage all aspects of your finances. These programs can help manage your donor or patron database, track your travel expenses, produce tax forms, generate detailed budgets. Programs like Fractured Atlas and software like DonorPerfect or Intuit Quickbooks (there is a nonprofit version) can help you navigate business and financial matters so that you avoid costly financial mistakes. As you know, business missteps can easily spell the end of your arts career. These programs, and others like them, cost money. You are either going to be purchasing software or paying a subscription fee for access to the material. However, in today's arts economy, we believe these business tools are not a frivolous luxury. They are essential components of your sustainable career in the arts. You would not think twice to spend valuable money on the necessary supplies for your art. You would gladly purchase audio equipment, new dance shoes, or paint brushes if you thought it would elevate your art. As an Artist Entrepreneur, you must adopt the same mindset for the business side of your enterprise. Spend the money to better manage your money.

Afterword

The central point of this book is to assist the emerging Artist Entrepreneur develop a sustainable career in the arts. Artists looking to utilize their talents to make a living have to go beyond the traditional college and university coursework in order to navigate the "new normal" in the arts industries. We have tried to shed some light on this new normal because talent alone is not enough to rise to the top of the supply chain within the crowded artistic landscape. We understand that emerging artists have to have their eyes wide open to the harsh realities of an arts career.

As Beeching says, you must go Beyond Talent. Great talent is just the baseline for an emerging artistic career. Creative artists must have an edge, an unwillingness to accept defeat, a "two steps forward, one step backward" mentality, and an awareness that finding work in the arts is a job. You have to know who you are, how to widely cast your net, and how to build a creative team of like-minded artists.

The core of our message is how a talented musician, actor, technician, painter, or writer can monetize and translate talent into a sustainable career. Young artists should understand the difference between a "fear-based education" with the return-on-investment that an advanced arts degree might provide. Within a competitive arts environment, emerging Artist Entrepreneurs must weigh the benefits of a graduate degree in the arts, such as artistic maturity and skill development, with the financial obligations and delay in starting a career.

The goal for the successful Artist Entrepreneur is a sustainable career and not living from gig to gig or being a flash in the pan. Successful Artist Entrepreneurs are visionary, collaborative, and creative. They understand and learn from being told "no," and how to find their inner creative soul.

The twenty-first-century Artist Entrepreneur understands that the arts are a big business that involves marketing, sales, and continuous self-improvement. The object is to work hard *and* smart. Finally, successful Artistic Entrepreneurs understand that a career in the arts is one of the most fulfilling careers in the world and our hope is that this book can help your dreams become reality.

Appendix A: Contract Example

This contract for one performance of The Artist's Project between the purchaser of music, _____ (herein called "**PURCHASER**") and the undersigned (herein called **ARTIST**) is made this day of _____.

Date(s): xxxxx

Shows/Time and Length: TBA/90 minutes

Number of Shows: One Show

Number of Artists: Four (4) Artists

Place of Engagement: xxxxx

Compensation Agreed Upon: xxxxx

Travel Fee Agreed Upon: N/A

Hotel Accommodations: N/A

Ground Transportation: N/A

PURCHASER will make payments as follows:

a. $xxx Deposit by check or money order payable to: **The Artist**
$xxx Balance due at the **conclusion of the performance** and hand delivered to The Artist. Please make check payable to: **The Artist**

b. Should PURCHASER cancel ARTIST after the signing date of this contract for any reason other than acts or regulations of public authorities, labor difficulties, civil tumult, strike, epidemic, interruption or delay of transportation service, or other similar or dissimilar cause beyond the control of either party, PURCHASER will compensate the ARTIST as follows:

c. Should the PURCHASER cancel before (insert date), the first payment of $xxx is due at the time of cancellation. Should the PURCHASER cancel after (insert date), the balance payment of $xxx is due at the time of cancellation.

PURCHASER will adhere to all requests in the attached Technical Rider.

In witness whereof, the parties hereto have hereunto set their names and seals on the date and year first above written.

X_____
Signature of PURCHASER
Representative

X_____
Signature of Signatory ARTIST

Appendix B

TECHNICAL RIDER EXAMPLE 1 (MUSIC)

The following rider represents the requirements of the Artists on the attached contract. *Please read it Carefully*. By signing it, you are agreeing to supply the Artist with certain equipment and working conditions, which are essential to the performance. Any breach of the terms of this contract is a breach of the contract and may cause the Artist to refuse to perform, without releasing you from the obligation to pay them.

We look forward to a smooth and successful engagement and would be happy to assist in any way. If there are problems in fulfilling any of these requirements, please call immediately. Please do not make any changes without permission from the Project Directors. Thank you for your cooperation.

A. Advertising and Promotion

A1. Billing on all advertising and publicity must appear as follows:

ARTIST PROJECT TITLE

A2. **ARTIST** is to receive 100 percent star billing on ALL publicity releases and paid advertisement, including without limitation: programs, flyers, signs, newspaper ads, marquees, tickets, radio, TV spots, etc., unless otherwise authorized by Artist of representative.

A3. **PURCHASER** agrees to use only artwork, ad mats, photos, and/or promotional materials provided or approved by Artist or representative.

A4. **PURCHASER** agrees not to commit Artist to any personal appearances, interviews, or other promotional or appearance without prior or written consent from the Artist or representative.

A5. **ARTIST** shall have the sole exclusive rights, but the not the obligation, to sell souvenirs in connection with and at the performance hereunder and the receipts thereof shall belong exclusively to Artist.

A6. **Artist** will assume all liability for Insurance.

A7. **Artist** will assume all tax deductions from fees.

A8. There are to be no other acts on the bill without the prior written consent of the artist.

A9. **ARTIST** shall not be required to appear or perform before any audience that is segregated on the basis of race, color, or creed, or where physical violence or injury to the Artist is likely to occur.

A10. **PURCHASER** agrees that there shall be no signs, placards, or other advertising materials on or near the stage during the entire performance, nor shall the Artist's appearance be sponsored by or in any other way tie in with any political candidate, commercial product, or business.

B. Travel, Dressing Rooms, and Catering

B1. Two (2) comfortable and private dressing rooms with clean lavatories, full-length mirror, table, chairs, garment rack, and waste bucket.

B2. Food and refreshments for five (5) people are to be prepared and inside the Artist's Dressing room by Artist's specified load-in time.

Pasta salad

One (1) fresh fruit/vegetable platter with dip

Assorted sandwiches with condiments on the side

Tea and coffee

Assorted fruit juices

Seven (7) liters of spring water

Ten (10) cans of assorted sodas (including Diet Coke) on ice

All necessary items (i.e., plates, napkins, etc.) for consumption of food specified above

Sufficient cups for beverages and on-stage drinks

Clean ice for drinks

Five (5) clean hand towels

B3. Hot meal, to be catered at the venue, for five (5) people. Time to be specified by Artist's representative. Suggestion: baked chicken, ribs, grilled salmon, steak, with appropriate dishes. No fast food, please!

B4. **PURCHASER** agrees to provide Artist's representative with detailed directions to the place of performance at least 14 days prior to date of performance.

B5. If **PURCHASER** is providing hotel accommodations, a minimum of four (4) single rooms are required. Purchaser shall not be responsible for any extra charges during the stay. Please list the name, address, and phone number of hotel provided. The hotel provided must be of four (4) star quality or higher for the Artist.

B6. **PURCHASER** will provide ground transportation for four (4) persons in a passenger van or other vehicle large enough to accommodate all passengers and luggage.

C. Sound and Lighting Requirements

C1. **PURCHASER** shall provide a professional sound and lighting crew to operate systems and assist with load in/set up/load out, and to work with artists for desired results.

C2. **PURCHASER** shall provide at his/her sole cost and expense a first-class professional sound reinforcement system with the minimum requirements as follows:

a. Adequate 1,500-watt sound system with 12-channel board with four (4) separate stage monitor mixes, pre-fade sends and two (2) post-fade sends, for effects. If a console with six (6) auxiliary sends is not available,

a separate on-stage monitor console should be supplied. Minimum three (3) band EQ on each channel and overall ⅓ octave EQ.
b. 1,500 watt House speakers
c. Microphones: 2 Shure Vocal Microphones (one for spoken word, one for trumpet/flute), 5 high-quality AKG, Sennheiser, Shure or equivalent, (2 for piano, 1 overhead for drums, 1 for snare, 1 for acoustic upright bass)
d. 5 working telescopes boom stands, with clips; or appropriate amplification for ensemble of five performers
e. Five (5) stage monitors
f. One (1) podium, with shielded lighting, for spoken-word performer
g. Audio CD player for musical preamble and intermission soundtrack

C3. Professional quality stage lighting.

C4. BACKLINE REQUIREMENTS:

a. One professional upright <u>acoustic bass</u> (1 fully carved no plywood or laminated instruments) ¾-size double bass, equipped with a *Realist* pick-up and an adjustable bridge). **UPON REQUEST**
b. One acoustic 7ft or 9ft *grand piano* tuned to a 440 day of show
c. A full drum kit, professional quality, Gretsch or Yamaha preferred. 18" bass drum, 12" × 8" rack tom, 14" × 14" floor tom, 14" × 5½" snare, two cymbal stands, one hi-hat stand, one snare stand, one bass drum pedal, one throne. **UPON REQUEST**
d. Four music stands with lights.

C5. VIDEO PROJECTION REQUIREMENTS:

a. Projection screen preferably rear projection and as large as possible (20ft or larger for full size professional auditoriums; 12 ft. absolute minimum for small-capacity [under 300] performance spaces); screen should be mounted/flown center stage behind band and podium; screen should be masked on all sides to wings, floor, and teaser height.
b. Video projection of necessary lumens/angle to fill screens and still provides a sufficiently bright image to cut through ambient concert lighting.
c. Video line to run videography from live computer (on stage) to projector (position will be determined after initial discussion with stage manager/tech director); video send will be S-video or DVI or VGA.

Appendix C

TECHNICAL RIDER EXAMPLE 2 (DANCE)

TECHNICAL RIDER of contract dated _____ between DANCE ARTIST (hereinafter called COMPANY), and _____ (hereinafter called PRESENTER).

The Technical Rider is of the essence of the Contract, and no portion may be waived or changed, and no addition made, without the express consent and signature of an authorized representative of DANCE ARTIST.

I. AVAILABILITY OF HALL

COMPANY requires the exclusive use of and shall be the sole occupant of the performance hall commencing at load-in and continuing through load-out. COMPANY requires access to the hall on the day PRIOR to the first performance activity. No other performances or rehearsals shall be booked in the Hall for the duration of the Engagement. Under no circumstances will the COMPANY be required to move or remove scenery, equipment, lighting, or other materials during the Engagement.

Work light and proper heat levels (70 to 75 degrees F) must be maintained in the performance area, backstage, and in dressing rooms and all other support spaces including but not limited to: studios, stairwells, elevators, green rooms, etc., for the duration of the engagement. PRESENTER agrees to make all necessary arrangements to control and regulate any air conditioning, heat, or temperature control systems so that the above heat levels can be maintained and excessive drafts and mechanical noise can be eliminated.

II. STAGE

Stage and all support spaces must be clean, swept, mopped, and cleaned of all debris prior to COMPANY Stage Manager arrival.

Stage should be a minimum of 40' wide at the proscenium opening and 30' deep from the curtain line to the most downstage of the upstage draperies to be used. Floor can be either natural wood or battleship linoleum, but must not rest directly on concrete. DANCE ARTIST RESERVES THE RIGHT TO CANCEL ANY PERFORMANCE SCHEDULED WHERE STAGE FLOOR IS CONCRETE OR LINOLEUM LAID DIRECTLY ON CONCRETE, OR WOOD LAID DIRECTLY ON CONCRETE.

The wing area and crossover space (at least three feet in depth) must be free of all scenery and equipment and be cleaned of all dirt and debris as well as adequately lit prior to arrival of COMPANY Stage Manager. If house has live stage video display capability please have set up prior to arrival for COMPANY Stage Manager down stage right. If infrared is a possibility please alert COMPANY.

Floor must be free of all nails, holes, cracks, splinters, waxes, gym-seal, and any other preparations that might make it slippery. Any repairs to holes and cracks should be sanded smooth.

COMPANY

PRESENTER

A black marley-type dance floor shall be provided by the PRESENTER at the PRESENTER'S expense. The dance floor must be laid prior to the arrival of the COMPANY Production Staff, and should be thoroughly mopped with ammonia or alcohol and water (not soap, or a soap and ammonia blend, as this makes the floor slippery), prior to the COMPANY'S arrival. Dancers must be allowed to wear character shoes and use rosin on the marley-type floor. Depending on Repertory, a white marley-type dance floor may be required in addition to the black.

One (1) table at least 6' in length and seven (7) chairs should be placed off-stage on each side prior to COMPANY arrival. In total, fourteen (14) chairs and two (2) tables. Company requires proper Ballet Barres for no less than 15 dancers.

III. CURTAINS AND MASKING
COMPANY requires the following:

—five (5) pairs of black legs
—five (5) black borders with no fullness
—one (1) full stage black scrim
—one (1) white or sky blue colored bounce drop (white preferred)
—one (1) seamless muslin or seamless plastic rear projection screen
—one (1) full stage black traveler, or full stage black drape, hung as far upstage as possible
—one (1) downstage main curtain

IV. SOUND
Venue to have all sound equipment in place prior to COMPANY arrival.

COMPANY requires the following:

—direct-input (DI) setup with ⅛-inch connection for COMPANY QLab
   Computer and 1–2 compact disk players for simultaneous primary QLab
   playback and backup playback. 2 simultaneous QLab playbacks is the
   COMPANY's preference. Please inform COMPANY Production Stage
   Manager (PSM) if an in-house QLab Setup is available as a sound operating method.
—mixer with separate adjustments for volume and equalization in the front
   of house speakers and the onstage monitor speakers
—speaker/amplification system capable of full range sound reproduction,
   with amplification commensurate with the size of the performance hall
—four (4) onstage monitor speakers, with amplification commensurate with
   the size of the stage
—one (1) microphone on a straight stand for lecture/demonstration performances; wireless is preferable
—two (2) Lavalier type microphones may be needed

An announcer's microphone must be provided backstage for use by the COMPANY PSM. For Technical Rehearsal please provide two (2) announcer's microphones at Tech Table FOH. If sound equipment must be rented, it must be set up in advance of the COMPANY'S arrival so that it may be tested early by COMPANY technical staff to determine if it is satisfactory. Sound control and level is at the COMPANY'S discretion, but every reasonable effort will be made to accommodate PRESENTER'S request.

A paging system from the stage manager's position to the dressing rooms must be provided.

V. INTERCOM SYSTEM
A closed-circuit intercom system is required to facilitate communication between COMPANY PSM (wireless or w/50ft cable), light booth, sound booth, follow-spot, fly crew, stage right and stage left. For Technical Rehearsal, please provide two (2) sets of com at Tech Table FOH. For performance, if a wireless headset is provided, please also provide a wired headset with a fifty (50) foot cable as a backup. If such system is not house equipment, it shall be rented by PRESENTER and installed prior to COMPANY load in.

VI. LIGHTING
DANCE ARTIST CARRIES NO LIGHTING EQUIPMENT AND WILL TAKE NO FINANCIAL RESPONSIBILITY FOR RENTAL OR OTHER PROCUREMENT OF SUCH EQUIPMENT AS STIPULATED HEREIN. Lighting equipment shall be provided by the PRESENTER and, if it is necessary to rent equipment, it shall be at the presenter's expense. The PRESENTER must provide a number of functional spares of each instrument type in case of unit failure.

All substitutions of equipment or alteration to the lighting plot must be approved by the company lighting supervisor.

Drawings and paperwork generated by the COMPANY Lighting Supervisor represent visual concepts and construction suggestions only. They do not replace the knowledge and advice of a licensed structural engineer or electrician. The COMPANY Lighting Supervisor is unqualified to determine the structural appropriateness of the provided design and will not assume responsibility for improper engineering or use.

The COMPANY's lighting plot must be hung, circuited, patched, and tested for full functionality prior to the arrival of the COMPANY technical staff. All installation must follow the most stringent safety standards both electrically and structurally.

All lighting positions be accessible during load-in, technical rehearsal, and show runs. All flying electrics must be cabled with sufficient slack so as to be able to fly into a working height for overhead color changes without hitting boom positions.

The COMPANY requires at least two-hundred-eighty-eight (288) 2.4kw dimmers and a ETC EOS family control console. The PRESENTER must provide the amperage needed to operate the lighting rig at its fullest possible electrical draw.

The COMPANY requires all non-boom color and all accessories to be provided and installed in units prior to COMPANY arrival. Templates and color for the boom color change will be provided by the COMPANY upon their arrival, with the PRESENTER providing frames and template holders.

The COMPANY requires the following lighting equipment. All of the equipment is to be supplied with appropriate lamp, gel/template frame, hanging hardware, connections, and safety cables so as to comprise a safe and functional system. All equipment is to be painted matte black.

LIGHTING UNITS

—five (5) ETC Source4 10°—750w
—ten (10) ETC Source4 15° —750w
—seventy (70) ETC Source4 19° —750w
—fifty (50) ETC Source4 26° —750w
—eighty (80) ETC Source4 36° —750w
—ten (10) ETC Source4 50° —750w
—fifty (50) ETC Source4 PAR WFL—750w OR PAR 64 WFL—1kw AND an
    assortment of MFL, NSP, and VSP lenses/lamps.

—twelve (12) 3-Cell Striplight—1kw/ cell (must comprise a wash across the full opening of the cyclorama)

ACCESSORIES

—twenty-four (24) Drop-in Iris for ETC Source4
—twenty-four (24) B-Sized template holder for ETC Source4
—twenty-four (24) A-sized template holder for ETC Source4

HARDWARE

—eight (8) 10' booms w/ appropriately secure bases
—fifty (50) 1' Sidearms w/ sliding tees

The PRESENTER must account for and provide all the necessary cable, power distribution, iron, stiffeners, bumpers, trussing, insulation, and rigging systems needed to safely hang the lighting plot as specified. The PRESENTER's staff must circuit the lighting plot so as to provide the control specified in the lighting paperwork.

Additionally, the PRESENTER must provide worklights for general illumination, and FoH units to act as curtain warmers (of an instrumentation and color most appropriate to the space). The PRESENTER must provide a red spotting light FoH on centerline, visible from the stage and as close to eye level as possible.

The COMPANY requires the PRESENTER to provide an up-to-date, annotated, and to-scale Vectorworks or CAD drawing of the performance space, complete with lighting positions, rigging systems, architectural obstacles, and descriptions any relevant idiosyncrasies of the space. The PRESENTER must provide an inventory of lighting equipment, control, dimming, hardware, etc. to the COMPANY Lighting Supervisor.

For the Technical Rehearsal, please provide a lighting tech table in the center of the house, complete with com (per Section V) and desktop lighting for illumination. The tech table must have at least 2 monitors able to display information from the light-board.

ADDITIONAL EQUIPMENT WILL BE REQUIRED, DEPENDING UPON REPERTORY.

COMPANY may require one followspot and trained operator.

VII. DRESSING ROOMS/PRODUCTION OFFICE
At least two separate dressing rooms are needed for seven men and seven women dancers, in addition to a private room for the Artistic Director with working phone and shower, and a room for COMPANY personnel. Each dressing room shall have: mirrors with adequate lighting, clothes racks with hangers, electrical outlets, table space, and wash basins with hot and cold running water. Toilet and shower facilities should be either in the dressing rooms themselves, or nearby. COMPANY requires 16 shower towels.

Dressing rooms and rest rooms must be separate and apart from public view and as close to the stage as possible. Audience members must not be able to enter the dressing room area, nor use the same toilet facilities as the dancers. Dressing rooms and toilet facilities should be cleaned thoroughly prior to the COMPANY'S arrival.

Room in the wings for quick changes will be needed on both stage right and stage left. Should certain repertory works be performed, a "quick change" booth may be required on stage left and stage right.

A Production Office is needed for the COMPANY Manager with a working phone line, internet access (either high speed or wireless), and a work station with a desk and chair. It is preferable for the Production Office to be within close proximity to the theater area and other COMPANY personnel. Access to a fax machine and a photocopier is also requested.

VIII. WARDROBE
COMPANY requires a large room convenient to the dressing rooms for use by COMPANY wardrobe director. Room must be well-lit with AC outlets for irons and sewing machines, and have at least four (4) rolling racks for hanging costumes. Washing machines, dryers, sinks for hand washing, steamer, and an iron and an ironing board, sixty (60) hangers, and four (4) laundry baskets are also required. If sewing machine is available please alert COMPANY Technical Director.

IX. STAGEHAND REQUIREMENTS

DANCE ARTIST is NOT a yellow card attraction. COMPANY travels with Production Stage Manager, Lighting Supervisor, Wardrobe Director, and in some cases, a Wardrobe Assistant.

Eight to ten experienced stagehands are required to work the load-in and set-up, depending on the theater. COMPANY'S minimum running crew consists of: one (1) sound person, one (1) light board operator, and up to five (5) stage hands that can work as electricians, prop persons, and flymen/carpenters. One house staffperson or crewperson should be available to function as a deck chief/ASM on the opposite side of the stage of the COMPANY PSM for purposes of communication and safety only. If the fly floor is not at stage level, more personnel may be required. Certain repertory may require additional personnel.

One (1) wardrobe assistant will be needed to prepare costumes prior to each performance, for the dress/technical rehearsal and show, and for load-out.

COMPANY requires sixteen (16) hours in the theater prior to curtain time of the first performance; eight (8) hours the day before the first performance or lecture/demonstration performance, and eight (8) hours on the day of the first performance. A spacing and full technical rehearsal with lights, sound, props, scenic, off-stage quick costume changes, and dancers will commence early afternoon on the day of the first performance of each program and will continue until dinner break.

Load-out will commence immediately following the final performance of the Engagement.

EXAMPLE OF TYPICAL PRODUCTION SCHEDULE:

First day—Load-in with COMPANY crew

9:00a–11:00a Unload truck, mark marley floors, insert templates and color, prepare and distribute costumes and dressing areas
11:00a–1:00p Begin focus, begin assembly of necessary props and scenery
1:00p–2:00p Lunch
2:00p–6:00p Resume focus and wardrobe & prop work, Soundcheck with PSM

Second day—Check cues and sound levels, Technical rehearsal, Performance, Strike

9:30a–12:30p LD looks at cues, PSM listens to sound levels (as needed following Day 1)
12:30p–1:30p Crew break while Company warms up onstage in worklight using boombox with iPod capability
1:30p–6:00p Show crew call—Technical Rehearsal
1:30p–2:00p Prepare stage and cues for Technical Rehearsal
(Company warm-up class completes onstage)
2:00p–5:00p Space and Run through of program with lights, sound, props, fly, and possibly costumes
5:00p–6:00p "Fix what needs fixing" without Company—reset stage
6:00p–7:00p Dinner break (stage available for Company self-warmup)
7:00p Show crew call—check sound and lights as unobtrusively as is possible
7:30p Half hour, House opens
8:00p–10:00p Performance
10:00p Strike begins
11:30p Equipment packed up into truck

IT IS ESSENTIAL THAT THE CREW WHO WORK THE LOAD IN AND TECHNICAL REHEARSAL BE THE SAME AS THOSE WHO WORK THE PERFORMANCE.

Stagehands may be non-union unless local regulations require that union stagehands be employed. PRESENTER agrees to employ and pay all stagehands, whether union or non-union, including loaders, if required.

PRESENTER and COMPANY agree that they will abide by all applicable rules and regulations of the labor unions and/or guilds having jurisdiction over the services in connection with the Engagement. COMPANY shall be notified of any union jurisdiction at least four (4) weeks in advance.

PRESENTER further agrees to provide one person with a good working knowledge of the facility, the authority to represent the PRESENTER with decision making power, to be present, responsible to, and accessible for consultation with COMPANY PSM at all times during the Engagement.

X. HOSPITALITY

On performance days and lecture/demonstration performance days when the COMPANY (20) is working in the theater, PRESENTER shall provide COMPANY with access to bottled water, assorted juice, packets of Emergen-C, a large pot of coffee, milk/cream, sugar, hot water w/tea bags, sliced lemons, fresh fruit, mixed yogurt, assorted pastries including bagels w/butter and cream cheese. Setup shall be in an easily accessible area backstage close to the dressing rooms, to be available beginning with the earliest arrival of COMPANY personnel. On regular performance days a hot meal and beverage service must be provided backstage for the COMPANY (20). PRESENTER and the Company General Manager will agree on the menu and time of meal service two (2) weeks before the COMPANY'S arrival.

XI. PROGRAMMING—(Please initial next to each line to confirm)

If Dance 1 is being performed a Hazer with fan will be required.

If Dance 2 is being performed, a grey Marley type dance floor will be required in addition to the standard black, and 3 "Mini-10" like "set" lights and haze will be required.

If Dance 3 is being performed a moving electric and haze will be required.

If Dance 4 is being performed 3 "Rosco-Icues" mirrors (or instruments with equivalent moving capacity) will be required. Haze is also required.

If Dance 5 is being performed, a white marley type dance floor will be required in addition to the standard black.

If Dance 6 is being performed, additional stage hands may be required to assist in removal/laying of additional flooring.

If Dance 7 is being performed, additional linesets for scenery and an additional fullstage black curtain in a downstage position will be needed. Additional stagehands may be required for simultaneous operation of multiple flying linesets. Additional shipping costs may be required for the scenic elements. Eleven (11) 8" Fresnel lighting instruments at 2kw, with barndoor accessories will be needed. Part of this ballet is danced in the aisles of the House orchestra and orchestra pit. Additional marley panels are required for covering the orchestra pit floor, as are hangable lighting positions to light the aisles and pit area while the curtain is closed. Front-of-house access must be available both over the stage and from the back of the house aisles without crossing over stage.

If Dance 8 is being performed additional linesets for scenery will be needed, as well as two (2) lengths of ¾-inch conduit bottom pipe, 10ft in length. One (1) "Mini-10" like "set" light and nine (9) 8"-Fresnel lighting instruments will be needed. Additional stagehands may be required for simultaneous operation of multiple flying linesets. Additional shipping costs may be required for the scenic elements.

If Dance 9 is being performed, an additional lineset for scenery will be needed. A wireless handheld microphone will be required for use onstage by the dancers. A hangable front-of-house position with a clear, flat front shot to upper ⅔ of cyclorama is also required.

If Dance 10 is being performed, three (3) additional linesets with the capability for the batten to move will be needed for electrics. Five (5) 8" Fresnel lighting instruments at 2kw, with barndoor accessories and 5 taildown pipes will be needed. A hangable front-of-house position with a clear, flat front shot to upper ⅔ of cyclorama is also required for three instruments.

If Dance 11 is being performed, an additional lineset with the capability for the batten to move will be needed for electrics. An additional set of 3-cell striplights will be required with a hang position for top-lighting the full width of the cyclorama. Haze is also required for this ballet.

If Dance 12 is being performed, an additional lineset with the capability for the batten to move may be needed for electrics. This ballet may require an additional set of black-panel softgoods for upstage entrances, depending on the depth of the stage. Haze is also required for this ballet.

If Dance 13 is being performed, one (1) "Mini-10" like "set" light and nine (9) 8"-Fresnel lighting instruments will be needed. Haze is also required for this ballet.

If Dance 14 is being performed a follow spot, haze and dry ice fog will be required.

Additional Dances may require a projector with enough size and brightness to, at a minimum, cover the entire cyc. Contact COMPANY PSM for further information.

AGREED TO AND ACCEPTED BY:
Federal ID#
By _____ Date _____

For PRESENTER:
By _____ Date _____

Appendix D

TECHNICAL RIDER EXAMPLE 3 (THEATER)

NOTE ABOUT THIS DOCUMENT:

The following document sets out the Technical Requirements and support to be provided to the Company by the Presenter.

Please be aware that any information herein is intended as a guide to the intended technical requirements and may be adapted to your venue's specifications.

Please contact us directly with any questions or issues arising from this document.

PRESENTING TEAM

Performers: × 5

Technicians: × 2 (Tour Manager, Company Manager)

In addition the Director and Designer may be required for the initial performance of any tour.

LOAD-IN/NUMBER OF PERFORMANCES

With a pre-rig of lighting and some audio elements as requested, the load in can be completed in three hours.

The load out takes approximately two hours.

Up to 8 performances are possible in a week that includes travel and load in.

Additional performances may be possible pending discussion of specific schedules.

RUNNING TIME

Approximately 55 minutes with no interval.

LATECOMERS POLICY

Latecomers can be admitted however we prefer they are seated at the back of the auditorium.

WARNINGS

Theatrical haze effects and Bubble Machine used from stage right. Bubble residue needs to be mopped up.

Theatrical Performance is recommended for audiences 5 years +

REQUIRED PERFORMANCE SPACE:

VENUE

Theatrical Performance is adaptable to most performance venues with the dimensions below, although is best suited to proscenium or end-stage theatre configurations with fly facilities. Alternative venue layouts without fly facilities are possible, but may require additional equipment. Please contact us to discuss.

STAGE AREA:

The show can be adjusted to fit onto a variety of stages of varying widths and heights, however the minimum stage dimensions are:

Proscenium Arch
Plaster line to US Curtain—29'6"
Plaster line to Lip of apron—6'6"

Opening of—29'6" with 6' of wing space on either side.
Height of proscenium –20'

STAGE SURFACE:

Flat surface (or raked stage with angle less than 1:12 rise) with no uneven areas. This can either be a raised stage area or set at audience level.

AUDITORIUM—STAGE ACCESS

As an essential element of the show, several audience members are invited to the stage by the presenter character called the Host. Theatrical Performance must be advised prior to the company's arrival if this is not possible due to either physical or policy reasons.

Six (6) Four (4) seats in the front row must be withheld from sale and reserved for pre-selected children.

If the stage area is raised, two sets of stairs (one set on each side) should be provided to easily facilitate audience stage entry. It is essential that front of house staff assist in children's entrance to the stage. Please station an usher at each set of stairs.

SET

The set consists of a custom-made curtain hanging immediately upstage of the proscenium, with a "decompression chamber" box sitting to one side on the stage left side.

Mid-stage there is a full-stage black drape, preferably rigged on a tab-track with a center opening. This should be operable from stage right.

An additional full-stage black drape hangs at the rear of the space.

Venue to Provide:

- Approved, recent, venue plans ideally showing both plan and section views.
- Full stage black drape or black wall upstage of the performance area.
- Preferred: Mid-stage 2 × half-stage black drapes on tab track or able to fly in and out. These should be rigged to create a centre opening. Note: If a split

black is not possible, 25' feet of wing space is required either stage left of stage right with 16' height clearance and 6' of depth.

- 25lb stage weights and shot bags.
- 30' tall × 10' wide black legs (This may be reduced depending on venue layout and size)
- Preferred: 1 Three (3) working battens ideally located 5' and 10' from the plaster line. Please send the typical lineset schedule in your theatre ahead of time so battens can be assigned for use.

Company to Provide:

- 30' wide × 20' high custom-made scrim used as a Kabuki drop Projection Screen. Should be able to fly out quickly. Show travels with a set of legs to be hung on the same lineset as the scrim.
- A Kabuki rig is available in the event that the venue does not have a working fly system or cannot guarantee that goods can be flown out quickly. If the Kabuki rig is to be used, either the assigned batten has to be able to fly in to the deck, or two lifts are available to attach the Kabuki rig to the pipe. When it is determined that the Kabuki drop will be used, the Kabuki rig must be installed, rehearsed, and restored by the half hour call or, in cases when a VIP Meet and Greet is scheduled, restore of drop must be complete 15 minutes prior to start of VIP Meet and Greet.
- All props and puppets required for the performance.
- Self-standing floor truss with lighting instruments and cable
- Company travels with all onstage lighting.

LIGHTING

It is expected that FOH lighting will be pre-rigged prior to the company's arrival.

In the event this is not possible an alternative schedule allowing for additional time will be required. Programmable house lighting (controllable from the operating position) should be provided.

A detailed lighting plan will be provided prior to the company's arrival at the venue.

Lighting is operated along with the audio-visual elements and the audio play-back by the touring Production Manager from stage right onstage.

Venue to provide:

- All equipment below run on a maximum of 2 DMX universes
- Programmable house lighting as described, to be run through a single dimming channel operated from the operating position or as a separate DMX channel.

Equipment list provided by Company:

- 14 × Wide Zoom profiles (e.g., ETC Source4 25-50)
- 6 × Narrow Zoom profiles (e.g., ETC Source4 15-30)"
- 2 × Iris to fit narrow zoom profile
- 36 × 10A individual dimmer channels Non-dim power
- 2 × DMX controllable Hazers (MDG Atmosphere with CO_2 Canisters preferred)
- 1× DF-50 Hazer
- All cables and DMX for the above

Alternatives to this can be discussed if the proposed is not suitable/achievable for your venue.

Company to provide:

- Nomad and QLab on one computer
- 1 × ENTTEC USB-DMX dongle
- 1–2 × Antari B200 Bubble Machine(s)
- 2× Bubbletron Bubble Machines

SOUND

Audio cues are operated by the Theatrical Performance team the front of house position described above.

The audio operation position must be within the auditorium onstage with no obstructions to the PA system.

The audio system and provided desk will need a venue technician to install and appropriately tune to the auditorium, and also to mix the live and pre-recorded elements throughout the performance.

Audio source is a Macbook Pro running QLab run through a MOTU Ultral-ite. Scarlett IO USB Audio Interface.

The two hosts require wireless headset microphones.

The following list of equipment is open to negotiation and substitution, within the parameters of a high quality performance sound system. All changes MUST be approved by the company prior to arrival at the venue.

Preferred brands are Meyer and/or d&b audiotechnik.

Venue to provide:

- Full Range, flown, left/centre/right front of house system with emphasis on clarity, precise coverage of entire audience area and reduced visible profile. Reinforcement of bass frequencies through separate subwoofer system is required. System should be capable of 115dbA undistorted sound at front of house operating position.
- 4 × Full-range left/right surround speakers (UPM-1P preferred) mounted above the rear of the auditorium.

Exact positioning to be determined upon receipt of venue plans.

- Left / Right onstage fold back
- All appropriate crossovers and drive to suit speaker system.
- All appropriate patch and speaker cable.
- 6 × 6.5mm jack–male XLR cable snake

Console:

- 1 × Digital audio console with 10in/8out minimum and on-board effects
- Note that analogue consoles will require additional outboard equipment.

Microphones (Provided by Venue):

- 2 × channels of Shure UR4+ with antenna system
- 2 × UR1M body packs

- 2 × DPA d:fine 66 (omnidirectional)
- Microphone belt packs
- These requirements may be substituted for in-house wireless headset microphones if available

Company to Provide:

- Macbook Pro running appropriate software
- MOTU Ultralite Mk 3 Scarlett IO to USB Audio Interface

AUDIO-VISUAL

Projection is all pre-recorded imagery, with operation by the touring Production Manager from within the auditorium at the same position as the lighting and audio elements.

Signal source is a Macbook Pro running QLab output to HDMI from front of house Tour Manager position.

Company to Provide:

- Macbook Pro running appropriate software
- Thunderbolt–HDMI adapter
- 1 × Barco RLS-W12 with zoom lens appropriate for venue. Panasonic R212K
- Rigging for projector
- HDMi cable from Front of House to projector (may need extenders)
- All associated power and signal cable

COMMUNICATIONS

4 × sets of communications are required.

2 × sets are at the front of house operating position (Production Manager and Sound Operator).

2 × wireless sets onstage (Stage Manager and Stagehand).

In addition, provisions should be put in place to ensure clear communication between the operating position and Box Office/Front of House.

WARDROBE:

Theatrical Performance travels with all appropriate costumes, however, suitable washing and drying facilities should be provided on-site. If there are no laundry facilities on-site then an alternative washing service (to be paid for by the presenter) should be arranged.

Venue to Provide:

- Suitable washing and drying facilities on site.
- An iron and ironing board or steamer.
- 2 × costume rack and 10 × coat hangers.

DRESSING ROOMS

Rooms required: 2 (1 × Female, 1 × Male)

These rooms must be secure and for the exclusive use of the company during the period of load in until the completion of the load out. Dressing room must be cleaned before arrival and throughout the season. Rooms require access to showers, toilets, hot and cold running water, at least 1 rack for hanging costumes, sufficient lighting, tables, chairs, bins, and mirrors.

HOSPITALITY RIDER

Venue to provide

- 6 × 1 liter bottles of still water per performance/rehearsal, or appropriate access to filtered water
- If venue schedule does not allow for meal breaks presenter will furnish a protein rich, nutritious meal with vegetarian, gluten-free alternatives.
- Company requests snacks including protein bars, fruit, yogurt, deli meats, wheat crackers, pita chips, Topo Chico water, and Neuro Waters. Snacks should include gluten-free, vegetarian options.

FREIGHT

Freight travels in five (5) eight (8) road cases on wheels, four (4) rolling dance towers, and three (3) hanging trusses. Please notify the company if there are likely to be difficulties with the easy access of these cases onto stage.

MERCHANDISE

Merchandise is for sale at public shows and travels in a self-contained display/ road case. Company provides seller.

INDICATIVE LOAD-IN SCHEDULE

The following schedule is designed with an opening on the evening of the first day.

This will not be possible unless all lighting and the main audio PA are pre-rigged.

LOAD IN/OUT CREW

Required crew numbers will be done by negotiation with each venue. This will be developed in conjunction with an appropriate production schedule. In general though it is expected that the venue will need to provide the minimum following crew:

Load-in (3hr Call)
1 × Lighting Op
1 × Audio Engineer
1 × Flyman
2 × Stagehands

Show Call
1 × Lighting Op
1 × Audio Engineer
1 × Flyman
2 × Stagehands

Load-out (2hr call)
1 × Lighting Op
1 × Audio Engineer
1 × Flyman
2 × Stagehands

All TERMS AGREED AND ACCEPTED

Purchaser / Venue Signature: _____ Date: _____

Artist or Authorized

Artist Representative Signature: _____ Date: _____

Appendix E

Itinerary

Langston Hughes Project

University of South Carolina, Western Carolina University,
Lander University, Arizona State University-East
January 29–February 3, 2005

Saturday, January 29
Ron
Depart: LAX, 8:05 a.m. (Delta Fl# 0774)
Arrive: Atlanta, 3:13 p.m.

Sunday, January 30/Monday, January 31
Eli, Dan and Larka
Depart: LAX. 11:55 p.m. (Delta Fl# 1475)
Arrive: Atlanta 6:56 a.m.

Monday, January 31
Ron will join Larka, Dan and Eli
Depart: Atlanta, 8:42 a.m. (Delta Fl# 1481)
Arrive: Columbia 9:50 a.m.

John and Eric
Depart: Minneapolis, 6:21 a.m. (Delta Fl# 1220)
Arrive: Atlanta, 9:57 a.m.

Depart: Atlanta 11:39 a.m. (Delta Fl# 0897)
Arrive: Columbia 12:41 a.m.

Concert Schedule
1:00 p.m.	Check into hotel
3:30 p.m.	Eric check video equipment
4:30 p.m.	Band and John Sound-check
5:30 p.m.	Dinner
7:00 p.m.	Concert, (University of South Carolina)

Tuesday, February 1
8:30 a.m.	Depart for Western Carolina University
11:00 a.m.	Masterclass
12:00 p.m.	Lunch
1:30 p.m.	Check into hotel
3:30 p.m.	Eric check video equipment
4:30 p.m.	Band and John Sound-check
5:30 p.m.	Dinner
7:00 p.m.	Concert (Western Carolina University)

Wednesday, February 2
9:30 a.m.	Depart for Lander University
12:00 p.m.	Lunch
1:30 p.m.	Check into hotel
3:30 p.m.	Eric check video equipment
4:30 p.m.	Band and John Sound-check
5:30 p.m.	Dinner
7:00 p.m.	Concert (Lander University)

Thursday, February 3
3:30 a.m.	Depart for Columbia (Airport)

Everybody
Depart: Columbia, 6:00 a.m. (Delta Fl# 4187)
Arrives: Atlanta, 6:59 a.m.

Depart: Atlanta 8:27 p.m. (Delta Fl# 0989)
Arrives: Phoenix, 10:52 a.m.

12:00 p.m.	Lunch
1:30 p.m.	Check into hotel
3:00 p.m.	Eric check on video equipment
4:00 p.m.	Band and John Sound-check (Possible Clinic)
5:30 p.m.	Dinner
7:00 p.m.	Concert (Arizona State University-East)

Friday, February 4
Ron Larka, Dan and Eli
Depart: Phoenix 8:17 a.m. America West 8:17a.m.
Arrive: LAX 8:40 a.m.

John
Depart: Phoenix 7:26 a.m. (Delta Fl#1525)
Arrive: Salt Lake City 9:04 a.m.

Depart: Salt Lake City, 10:10 a.m. (Delta Fl# 4832)
Arrive: Minneapolis, 1:43 p.m.

Depart: Atlanta, 2:00 p.m. (Delta Fl# 0754)
Arrive: Newark, 4:07 p.m.

Sunday, February 6
Eric
Depart: Phoenix, 2:22 p.m. (Delta Fl# 4053)
Arrive: Salt Lake City 4:01 p.m.

Depart: Salt Lake City, 5:05 p.m.(Delta Fl# 1172)
Arrive: Minneapolis, 8:47 p.m.

Contact Information:
Ms. LaNea' Briggs
Student Activities Coordinator
University of South Carolina

Ms. Tanisha Jenkins
Student Activities Coordinator
Western Carolina University

Mr. Steve Hopkins
Student Activities Coordinator
Lander University

Mr. Mike Meader
Student Activities Coordinator
Arizona State University-East

Dr. Ron McCurdy

Dr. John Wright

Hotel Information
University of South Carolina
Best Western
1301 Main Street
Columbia, SC 29201
(803) 779-7790

Western Carolina University
Holiday Inn Express
26 Robinson Rd
Dillsboro, NC 28725
(828) 631-1111

Lander University
Best Western
5009 Pelham Rd
Greenville, SC
(864) 297-5353
Confirmation # 8791

Arizona State University-East
TBA

References

INTRODUCTION

Angela Beeching, *Beyond Talent: Creating a Successful Career in Music* (Oxford: Oxford University Press, 2010).

Daniel J. Wakin, "The Juilliard Effect: Ten Years Later" (*New York Times*, December 12, 2004).

Burning Glass Technologies and Strada Institute for the Future of Work (2018), "The Permanent Detour: Underemployment Long-Term Effects on the Careers of College Grads," https://www.burning-glass.com/research-project/underemployment/

CHAPTER 1

Facts and Figures Concerning Music and Higher Education in the United States, The College Music Society, 2015, https://www.music.org/pdf/mihe/facts.pdf

http://www.johnclaytonjazz.com/

http://justindicioccio.com/

Steven R. Covey, *The Seven Habits of Highly Successful People* (Free Press, 1989).

CHAPTER 2

Mihaly Csikszentmihalyi, *Creativity: Flow and the Psychology of Discovery and Invention* (New York: Harper Collins, 1996).

CHAPTER 3

"IBM 2010 Global CEO Study: Creativity Selected as Most Crucial Factor for Future Success," 2016.

Bureau of Labor Statistics, "Which Industries Need Workers? Exploring Differences in Labor Market Activity," January 2016. bls.gov/opub/mlr/2016/article/which-industries-need-workers-exploring-differences-in-labor-market-activity.htm

Jon Hamilton, "Think You're Multitasking? Think Again," NPR, 2008.

Ed Catmull, *Creativity, Inc.: Overcoming the Unseen Forces That Stand in the Way of True Inspiration* (New York: Random House, 2014).

Rebecca Greenfield, "How Disney's Imagineers Keep the Magic Ideas Coming," Fast Company, 2014.

CHAPTER 6

TheArtGuide.com

Jeri Goldstein, *Managing Your Own Career*, 2017.

CHAPTER 7

https://vlany.org/

Donald S. Passman, *All You Need to Know about the Music Business* (New York: Simon and Schuster, 2015).

CHAPTER 8

Hersey, P., Blanchard, K. H., & Natemeyer, W. E. (1979). "Situational Leadership, Perception, and the Impact of Power," *Group & Organization Studies, 4*(4), 418–28. https://doi.org/10.1177/105960117900400404

Richard E. Goodstein, "An Investigation into Leadership Behaviors and Descriptive Characteristics of High School Band Directors in the United States." *Journal of Research in Music Education.* Vol. 35, No. 1 (Spring, 1987), pp. 13–25.

Robert K. Greenleaf, *Servant Leadership: A Journey into the Nature of Legitimate Power and Greatness* (New York: Paulist Press, 1977).

CHAPTER 9

Gail Z. Martin, *The Essential Social Media Marketing Handbook* (New Jersey: Career Press, 2017).

http://www.clairbremnerart.com/

https://www.rankytanky.com/

https://www.okeedokee.org/

Index

graduate degrees/schools, 14, 129–30.
  See also education
grant funding, 119–24
Greenleaf, Robert K., 90
grit and determination, 32–33, 37–38,
  92–93

Hancock, Herbie, 11
Hersey, Paul, 89–90
hospitality requirements, 146, 156
humility, 97

illegal drugs, 117
imitation, 98
Impact Report, 124
initiators, 17
inspiration step of creative process, 46
Instagram, 105
intellectual artists, 15, 16
intellectual property, 86
intercom system requirements, 140
interviews, 112–14
itinerary, 115

jazz music, 39
jobs and relationships, 38–39
journals, 43, 47
Juilliard Effect (Wakin), 8, 59
Jump Swing, 57

Lapin, Eric: on "big fish, small pond"
  syndrome, 5; on creative process,
  44, 47; on flow, 27; on focus, 12; on
  getting paid, 49; on health and well-
  being, 12, 96; on lacking a plan, 15;
  on presenters' point of view, 71, 78,
  82, 83
lawyers, 65–66, 85–86, 111. *See also* legal
  agreements; technical riders

leadership: about, 87–89; management
  habits *versus,* 17–18; situational,
  89–90, 97; theories of, 89–91; traits of
  successful artists, 17–19, 91–99
League, Michael, 18
legal agreements: contracts, 110–11;
  costs, 81; "out" clause, 66;
  partnerships, 85–86; sample
  contracts, 131–32; sunset clauses, 64;
  technical riders, 111. *See also* lawyers;
  technical riders
lighting requirements, 135–36, 140–43,
  152–53
Limited Liability Corporation (LLC),
  116
LinkedIn, 105
LLC (Limited Liability Corporation),
  116
Lomazov, Marina, 2, 3, 22, 23, 70, 96
luck, 23

MailChimp, 107
mailings, 76–77, 106–7
managers, 61–62, 78
marketing process, 101–2, 106–7. *See
  also* social media
Marsalis, Wynton, 39
Matthews, Dave, 17
McCurdy, Ron: on artistic teams,
  64–65; on assessing prospects, 31; on
  business and professional work, 49,
  53, 54; on education, 14, 16, 20, 44;
  on quiet time, 42; on unpredictability
  of success, 51, 52; on vision, 58
McElroy, Michael: on artistic ownership,
  55, 102, 109; on artistic teams, 62, 68;
  on education, 5; on honing skills, 12,
  50; on musical background, 29
mentors, 20–21, 23, 95

About the Authors

Ronald C. McCurdy is professor of music in the Thornton School of Music at the University of Southern California (USC), where he served as chair of the jazz department for six years (2002–2008). Prior to his appointment at USC, he served as director of the Thelonious Monk Institute of Jazz at USC (1999–2001). He is co-author of a vocal jazz improvisation series titled *Approaching the Standards*. McCurdy wrote, *Meet the Great Jazz Legends* and contributed chapters to two recent publications: *Teaching Music in Performance through Jazz: Vol. I* and *African Americans and Popular Culture*. McCurdy is a consultant to the Grammy Foundation educational programs, including serving as director of the National Grammy Vocal Jazz Ensemble and Combo. McCurdy serves as a consultant and Artistic Board Member to YoungArts. He also serves as director of the Walt Disney All-American College Band in Anaheim, CA. http://www.ronmccurdy.com

Richard E. Goodstein is professor of music at Clemson University and dean emeritus of the College of Architecture, Arts and Humanities. He has been on the Clemson faculty since 1982 and during his tenure at Clemson, he has served as director of the Tiger Marching Band, director of bands, and chair of the Department of Performing Arts. Goodstein served as music director for a number of theatrical productions, such as *Rent, Marat/Sade, A Funny Thing Happened on the Way to the Forum, The Music Man, Urinetown,* and the 2010 Clemson University Capital Campaign Kick-Off. He also supervised the original score for *The Decameron Project*, an award-winning theatrical production that traveled to the International Fringe Festival in Edinburgh, Scotland. In addition to his work at Clemson, Goodstein is a consultant for the Walt Disney Co. and served for 11 years as the musical director of the Walt Disney World All-American College Band.

Eric J. Lapin is the director of artistic initiatives for the Brooks Center for the Performing Arts and a senior lecturer of music in the Department of Performing Arts at Clemson University. He teaches courses in applied clarinet, arts administration, and jazz history. As a clarinetist, Lapin has performed with the Piccolo Spoleto Festival Orchestra, the Spartanburg Philharmonic, the Limestone College Wind Ensemble, and has given solo performances for the Greenville Music Teachers Association and the 2012 Clemson University Victor Hurst Academic Convocation. Lapin has presented papers at numerous conferences, hosted research exhibits, published scholarly essays, and was recently named February 2017 Researcher of the Month by the Clemson University Library. In addition, Lapin also serves as a delegate to the Faculty Senate, is a member of the South Carolina Humanities Speaker's Bureau, is on the board of directors for the Pendleton Historic Foundation, and is on the University STEAM committee.

CPSIA information can be obtained
at www.ICGtesting.com
Printed in the USA
LVHW031659290120
645190LV00005B/481